Bufano

An Intimate Biography

Bufano in his studio in reflective mood.

Bufano
An Intimate Biography

 BY H. WILKENING
AND SONIA BROWN

BERKELEY · Howell -North Books · CALIFORNIA

BUFANO — An Intimate Biography

Printed and bound in the United States of America

Library of Congress Catalog Card No. 72-79789

ISBN 0-8310-7089-7

Published by Howell-North Books

1050 Parker Street, Berkeley, California 94710

' Contents

"And the least of his acts are works
of grace" —Henry Miller

ʹ Introduction

In 1943, when I began collecting material for this biography, I asked Benny how he would like it to be treated — as a straight biography or in a fictional-biographical form. "Any way you want," he said. "But maybe it would be best to tell it the way I look to the rest of the world, and then at the end have me kneeling in a confessional telling all my sins and all my truths.

"I might tell the same experience in different ways to my mother, to my father, to each of my brothers, to Fleishhacker, to Saroyan, to Will Rogers, Jr., to President Roosevelt, to Eleanor, to Harry Hopkins, to Sun Yat-sen, to Mahatma Gandhi, to J. Edgar Hoover, to Mrs. Whitney, and to you. And if each of you got together and repeated the story I had told, not only wouldn't you recognize the story, but you would all call me a damned liar. And, of course, I wouldn't be. I just told each person not only what I thought he wanted to hear, but I related it in the way I thought appropriate for him.

"So do what you want, as long as you tell the truths about me." He chuckled as he said, "Nobody'll believe anything you say about me anyway."

Many people have attempted to write Bufano's biography, or a reasonable facsimile thereof. It took persistent effort for more than twenty years to collect the information upon which this biography is based. Benny was kind enough to write to his friends for the originals of his letters, and he re-collected materials he had sent to other would-be biographers. When it was all brought together these data occupied a space equivalent to a room four feet square and eight feet high, with other memorabilia scattered throughout the State of California for use when needed. Between 1958 and 1963 thousands of dollars were spent in having this library categorized, penciling in marginalia and tabulating as complete a record of his works as possible. But there were still so many gaps.

In 1963 Benny was pinned down, almost roped, for week after week as he answered question after question that we put to him. All of his answers were tape-recorded and transcribed, so that as much as possible this story of his life is his, as he described it and in his words. Every comment attributed to Benny in this story either has been recorded and retyped or was prepared by him for speeches and radio and television interviews. The reader should assume, however, that whenever Benny discusses a subject, he is talking to the authors, unless specific reference is made to a newspaper article or magazine story in which Benny was interviewed.

In preparing Benny's story we have attempted to be authentic and precise, but to claim anything more than an attempt would not be the truth. Most people believe that if they have a date, they have a fact. Benny, of course, couldn't believe in such a myth. In most cases he felt that dates, details and directions were unimportant. What difference does it make if a man goes to China from California or New York, as long as he gets to China? What difference if a man created a work of art at the age of fifteen or seventeen? It was done during adolescence. It is not the details, but what a man did, what he stands for, that are important.

But it was also important, in preparing this work, to have some accurate names and dates that would give structure to such an elusive, mercurial character as Benny Bufano. And some people do care about relative facts and figures, so for these people — and for our own consciences — we spent considerable time and effort to verify many facts in Benny's story.

Benny proved to have an amazingly good memory, except for his own birth date. No one but a statistician or a mortician, Benny felt, would really care whether he was born in 1894, 1898, 1900 or 1910. As he got older, Benny agreeably changed the year, but only in favor of a later one. On occasion he obliterated the date altogether, as he did when autographing the beautiful book of his works published by the Bufano Society of the Arts. By considering all our interviews with Benny, information from his relatives in New York and gleanings from early newspapers, the date we arrived at for his birth was October 14, 1898. It is certainly as good a date as any.

During our taped interviews Benny would often say something that sounded questionable, and we would want to know as many facts as possible — names, dates, addresses — and to hear the other side of the story. This was not Benny's way. "My work speaks for itself. That's the only honesty. What I say is shit, and what others say is double shit." But after a bit of persuasion he might agree to provide the necessary information.

The Bulganin incident was one that sounded a little far-fetched. We contacted one of the educators who had toured the Soviet Union with Benny. He had dinner with us, and his story not only confirmed Benny's statements but provided us with even more startling information about this man to whom everything seemed to happen. And when it didn't happen to him as a matter of course, Benny went out and gave the Fates a prod.

I had known Benny since the 1940s, when we both worked under the F.H.A. We used to take long walks together, talking about almost anything but mostly about Benny himself. Since I am a trained psychologist, he would joke about my being his "therapist" and say that maybe he should be paying me a fat fee. I learned quite a bit about how he thought and felt during these relaxed conversations.

When Benny visited the Browns at their home in Los Angeles he would stay for days at a time. Whenever he arrived he went straight to the guest room, where he deposited his luggage — a paper shopping bag containing an extra pair of socks, a box of cleansing tissues, a nightshirt and three Little Blue Books.* Each night he washed one pair of socks and hung them in the window to dry. One wonders what the Browns' fashionable neighbors

---

*The Little Blue Books provided literary classics and popular reading matter for five cents each. They were early paperbacks, tiny enough to tuck into luggage or a handbag.

must have thought when they saw those socks — the "house flag" of their artist-in-residence.

The last major exhibit of Bufano's work, before his death, came in 1967 when S. Jon Kreedman wanted one of his statues for the lobby of his new office building at One Wilshire Boulevard. One statue? He didn't know Benny.

As Kreedman told it later, "It took four large moving vans to effectuate the shipment . . . and four different pieces of equipment to move the large objects into the bank and lobby of the building." During the first day, the building was jammed with television equipment, reporters and visitors. "It was almost necessary to close the bank for fear of damaging his works. . . . You wouldn't believe the mobs that were here. And anyway," said Mr. Kreedman, laughing, "we didn't want the public to think that there was a run on a new bank."

On a large poster, indicating the legend of Bufano, his birth date was listed as 1896. "That's a lie," said Benny. "Change it to 1910."

"Okay," Kreedman said, "the first thing in the morning."

The next day Kreedman arrived an hour earlier than usual to change the date for Benny, but Benny had beat him to it. He had also gone into Kreedman's office and changed a similar date in the book of Bufano's works that was on Kreedman's desk.

During the five years preceding his death, many people noticed that Benny was growing more irritable and distraught. He seemed to sense that he had so little time to get all his plans in operation. Kreedman related a few other incidents that occurred during the show. In one instance he had made arrangements to meet Benny at his home before going out to dinner, but Benny was more than an hour late, so the dinner party left without him. The next day Benny was furious, saying that he had gotten lost and had no money to get around. He was so irate that he demanded all his works be returned to San Francisco. But when Kreedman said that since that was Benny's wish he would be glad to comply, then Benny calmed down and went on with the show. At another time an elderly woman wanted to talk to Benny, but he told her, "Leave me alone. I'm too busy."

Benny added to his poverty-stricken appearance by wearing the same clothes for years on end. For one three-year stretch he wore nothing but a blue, short-sleeved polo shirt with baggy blue pants to match. According to Kreedman, "he dressed in that same plaid shirt, the same red tie and the same herringbone sport coat" during his month's stay in Los Angeles. He took a shower every day, however, and pressed deodorant out of a can onto his clothes. He seldom wore underwear. From all reports, Benny had the same habits at seventy that he'd had at twenty. He always seemed too busy to bother with clothes, yet on some special occasion he might show up in a fancy outfit, but one that did not quite fit. "Wearing clothes is a waste of time," Benny often said. "We should all go naked." But, as many of his friends knew, few people had ever seen Benny naked.

Benny worked like a demon for eight days and nights to set up the exhibit. "All during the first two weeks," said Kreedman, "he had spent his time in the bank giving out autographs, posing for pictures and talking to the public, describing his work. How proud and delighted this little tower of strength appeared!"

Is it possible to tell what sort of personality a man has from a judgment of his works? Or, knowing the man, can one guess the sort of work he might produce? You can make an interesting game out of these questions. Benny would have loved to play such a game with you. In one breath he would tell the pope that he rejected the phoniness of Catholicism, yet he clamored to be photographed with the pope. He loved kids — as he called them — and all kids loved him, yet he denied the existence of his own children. He was a man who despised money and what it stood for, yet he reveled in the company of the wealthy; a man who violently hated commercialism, yet permitted newspaper reporters to commercialize him. When his art was appreciated Benny became amenable, pleasant and co-operative, yet when things didn't go his way he was intractable, stubborn and manipulative. He was a man of such colossal ego and so calculating that nothing seemed to penetrate his thickened skin, yet he was so sensitive, so loving, so tender that tears came to his eyes as quickly as laughter to his lips.

I know a good name for him, you say. Yes, but hold it. You're wrong. You don't have all the facts. One name, one word or a million will never be enough. For one Benny, maybe. But never for the Benny of a thousand selves.

This biography is Benny's story, as the world knew him through articles and interviews, and as he told it to us, his biographers. At the end, in the Epilogue, are some of the "truths" that Benny told me privately. This is the Benny that others will call a liar. But they knew Benny as he wanted them to know him. And probably so did I.

HOWARD WILKENING

Los Angeles
November, 1971

1 · San Francisco and New York

It was 1914. Benny Bufano already showed signs of great talent. Before he was finished with his life work, many people would acknowledge that his sculpture was the most "significant contribution during the past five hundred years." He was seventeen years old.

The young Bufano looked Italian. His slim body, five feet tall, was lithe and muscular. His features were small; his blue eyes, deep set, were bright and alert; his head was well shaped and crowned by a bush of curly dark hair. He wore his shirts with the collars turned under and open at the throat. The sleeves were rolled up to be out of his way while he worked, and his loose trousers were always well spattered with the white plaster-like materials he was working with. He was good to look at and people liked him because of his ready smile, his sense of humor and quick wit.

He knew little of the world and its chicanery, and now he was to learn something about legal contracts. For the rest of his life the law and lawyers would haunt him, almost destroy him. He had never heard of Blackstone, who in his usually clear and lucid words had defined a contract as "an agreement, upon sufficient consideration, to do or not do a particular thing."

Bufano's first experience with the law had been the time he had been caught *flagrante delicto,* for indecent exposure when he was six years old. Ever since the incident he had hated authority. When he told of the episode he grinned and his eyes flashed. He always modified the story by saying that it's not the police who are cruel, they're just doing their duty. Mostly it's politicians that wreak havoc in the life of a man.

At six Bufano had lived on Sullivan Street in New York with his mother, Lucrecia, his father, Canio, and his fourteen brothers and sisters. Sullivan Street was the heart of Greenwich Village; it was a slum area that could easily have passed for a street in any Italian city where families of the poor made their home. Sullivan Street ran into Washington Square and the children played in the park. In the center of the square was a large circular fountain, about thirty feet in diameter, which squirted cold water. It was forbidden to bathe in this fountain but on hot, sweltering summer days the children figuratively thumbed their noses at the stupid, adult-inspired prohibition. On this particular day, keeping a sharp lookout for the cops, the boys stripped and plunged into the cool waters, splashing and jumping about. Suddenly the cops appeared.

"Jiggers."

Benny was so small he couldn't climb over the fountain wall fast enough, so a policeman grabbed him while the older boys ran and hid, leaving tiny Benny to take the rap. Bufano always remembered the humiliation of walking through the streets naked except for a cop's hat covering his middle. And he never forgot the blessed feeling when his mother came, her dark eyes flashing anger at the police, and found him huddled on a bench covered by a large blanket which a kindly officer had thrown over the small frightened boy. Lucrecia wrapped Benny in her shawl and led him home by the hand, comforting him with gentle words as they went. There was bitterness in Lucrecia and an unbearable nostalgia for her home in the village of San Fele, where children could play and roam the streets and even get into mischief without the cops dragging them into the police station.

But all this had happened eleven years before. Now, at seventeen, Bufano had already served his apprenticeship with the greatest and most famous sculptors of his time: Rafaelo Ranieri, the famous Sicilian carver of wood; Herbert Adams, the founder of the National Sculpture Society and famous for his portrait busts; and James Fraser, renowned for his *End of the Trail* and the buffalo nickel. They had all contributed to the genius of the talented young sculptor.

It was September of 1914 and the famous American sculptor, Paul Manship, had gotten a commission to make two sculptures for the Panama-Pacific International Exposition to be held the following year, 1915, in San Francisco. Manship, at the height of his career, had many other commissions and didn't have the time to go to San Francisco. He had completed the models for the exposition but the copies in plaster could be done by a good craftsman.

One day, as he stopped to buy a newspaper from Benny, Manship asked him if he would like to work part-time on a special job. Bufano accepted with his usual alacrity, asking when he could start; the sculptor smiled at Benny's youthful readiness and told him to come to his studio the following day. Manship knew of Bufano's apprenticeship with Ranieri, Adams, Martiny and Fraser, and had heard of his remarkable talent from these great sculptors. Benny gave his corner to his brother, who wanted to sell papers, and arrived at Manship's studio in Greenwich Village early the next morning. Manship had lined up Bob Paine to do the enlargements as he was an expert in this work. It was Bob who had suggested Bufano for the Ranieri modeling.

The following month Bufano and Paine left for San Francisco. It was a happy young Bufano who came to San Francisco carrying the two-and-a-half-foot scale models, like twin children, in his arms. He was ready to work hard and eager to see the sights.

He rented a room in one of the alleys off Grant Avenue in the middle of Chinatown. During the day he and Bob Paine worked on the Manship models. The evenings were spent browsing about San Francisco's Chinatown, where they were attracted by the shops filled with beautiful Chinese art objects: carved jades and soapstone, lacquered boxes exquisitely painted in gold, green glazed tiles carved and decorated, and oxblood vases whose glazes reflected the light in their rich reds, gladdening the heart of the young artist. He saw the carved stone Kuan Yins and gods, graceful figurines of carved ivory and pewter candlesticks of magnificent design; all these wonders of Chinese art were a never-ending delight to him. He promised himself that some day he would visit China and bring back its treasures. At seventeen everything in life seems possible, even the impossible.

Ying Choy, a young Chinese artist, a painter, lived in the room next to Bufano, and almost immediately they became friends. Ying was about to be married; so in his spare time Bufano began work on a wedding gift. On the day of the wedding he presented it to the couple — a sculptured group of the two young people, done in blue glazed stoneware. Years later the Metropolitan Museum of Art bought the *Honeymoon Couple*. In referring to this purchase the journal *International Studio* in February, 1925, said:

> They stand together aloof yet intimate, charming persons but something more than that, the essence of the high principled domesticity that Confucius enjoins and the Chinese poets have for two thousand years and more descriptively extolled. They are, moreover, not two persons but genuinely a group, unified by the relations of masses and the flow of draperies. And they are covered with fresh and lustrous glazes that have a moist translucency.
>
> The Chinese pieces are fine decoration and, what is more important, they are truly sculptural decoration.

By the time he had completed the *Honeymoon Couple* Bufano had fallen in love with San Francisco and had come to a decision. He would give up the precious studio he had only recently acquired in Greenwich Village and make his home in San Francisco. The thought of giving up his studio was a pain that wrenched at his heart. His first studio! Then there would be the parting from his mother Lucrecia, from his father Canio (this would not be so hard) and from his brothers and sisters. But on the other hand he loved the old streets of San Francisco with their subtle color of ancient brick and cobblestones, the harbor with its activity, the woods and the views of the sea. He loved Fisherman's Wharf, where he could talk to the fishermen in his native Italian, and above all he loved Chinatown.

San Francisco was a mixture of the old and new. It was only nine years since the old city had been destroyed by fire and earthquake. There were still spots where naked brick chimneys stood like ancient ghosts, a reminder of that holocaust. But on the whole the city had been rebuilt. Bufano loved to watch the cable cars with their turn-around stations, loved to imagine the picturesque people of the 1800's with their crinolined women and high-hatted men, the criminal element and the snobbery. The name of the city made him remember the stories his mother had told him of St. Francis and his goodness, and Bufano wanted this city, named after the saint, to be as good and pure of heart. The hills particularly enthralled him, and the vision came to him of a great statue standing high on one of them, its eyes overlooking the magnificent bay. This dream was born in the young artist and was never to leave him, bringing with it sorrow and disappointment.

He enjoyed talking with Ying Choy, his artist friend. They talked philosophy and art. Young Bufano gulped knowledge avidly and Ying was an educated man.

One day Bufano asked Ying to draw a bird. Ying did so with a few strokes of his brush, and with each stroke he sang a line of melody. Bufano was enchanted because he too always sang when he worked. It was at this time that Bufano said, "If you were to ask the artist for a definition of his work, why this or why that? . . . Ask the birds why they sing."

The young artist became articulate with Ying. They spoke of art and Bufano developed a thesis of his own: "Art is the people's one world . . . one color, one race. It is the only universal language spoken . . . cherished by every people or race on earth. It is the basic alphabet of human communication. Yet there are people who want to play around with that perfect alphabet, who want to reform all art. Art is not to be tampered with.

"Art comes to us as naturally as the rain falls, as the bird sings. We put the little seed into the earth, the seed sprouts to a plant. The plant gives forth the bud. Then the bud blooms and the blossom gives back the seed, and the seed goes back to the earth. If we would only let it, life itself could be almost as simple for the human. But the human is too mixed up to let things alone. He must improve, he must do over, he must reform without ever taking time out to discover if things or people really want to be improved, or gone over, or reformed.

"Through reforming we by no means rise to a more enlightened state of being. Reforming is but a stupid, sentimental human weakness. We do not need to reform, but to be transformed."

Benny's work at the exposition was so outstanding that the supervisor asked him to do some large panels for the Arches of Triumph. This was extra, original work which had nothing to do with the Manship contract. Then Maybeck, the well-known architect who was designing the Palace of Fine Arts, asked Benny to do a panel over the main door. Bufano would do a bas relief festoon over the door, in keeping with the Greco-Roman style of the building. Benny saw himself a plutocrat with the extra money he expected to be paid.

There was a deadline for completion set by the exposition contractors, but Benny, with Wagnerian disdain, had his own deadline. The official deadline came and Benny wasn't finished. The contractors complained that he was taking too much time. Bufano argued: he wanted his work to be perfect. The authorities countered that the plaster panels were just temporary and only needed to give the effect for the time of the exposition. This wasn't Bufano's way of working; anything he did had to be done to the best of his ability and the authorities could go hang! They threatened to stop paying him the two dollars a day he was getting, so he said, "To hell with the two dollars. I have to do the work right! No work of art should be temporary. It must be eternal."

Benny, five feet tall and slender, continued to stand high on the scaffolding before the Arches of Triumph and stubbornly continued his work. Very carefully and meticulously he carved the enormous panels, while singing the "Serenade" from *Don Giovanni* at the top of his voice: "Deh! vieni alla finestra." His bushy dark curls were rumpled by the strong San Francisco winds; his eyes were filled with the joy of his work and the prospect of making some extra money, in addition to the two-dollar-a-day stipend he was paid for enlarging Manship's two groups, *Poets* and *Musicians*.

The *Honeymoon Couple* was created in 1914, of blue glazed stoneware; the piece is in the Metropolitan Museum of Art, New York.

The young Bufano poses with his *David*, done in cast stone in 1915.
The ten-foot statue was destroyed during World War I.

Bufano was completely innocent about the hard realities of the business world and had no doubts about the fairness of people. Before leaving San Francisco, Benny would have been initiated into the first of his many bitter experiences in the complex world of legal hocus-pocus. When the exposition opened on February 20, 1915, Benny had finished his work. Only then did he ask to be paid for the panels on the Arches of Triumph and the festoon over the main door of the Palace of Fine Arts. The authorities reminded him that he had no contract!

"Contract!" He had never heard of such a thing. He had done the work and ought to be paid! To hell with a contract!

Without a contract, the authorities could no nothing about it.

But they had paid Manship for his work.

That was different. He had a contract. They refused to pay more than the two dollars per day, just like any other day labor.

Beniamino forced back the tears of disappointment, went to his room and shut the door. He had held within himself the tearing desire to cry out, to shout and tell the world about the great injustice of the officials. They had taken from him the weapon he needed against his father, who never missed the chance to tell him how stupid he was to be an artist. All the time Bufano had worked on the festoons he had imagined himself proudly entering his parents' flat and throwing down a large sum of money to help Lucrecia with the expenses of the family. Now all this was over. He had no money and he must face his father. Bufano threw himself on his cot and wept bitterly until the tears would come no more. At least he'd done a good job. He hadn't prostituted himself by hurrying. He would leave this rotten city forever. And some day he would show his father. He'd become famous, but he'd never sell out for money.

Later in life, when other disappointments had come to him, Bufano said in a press interview: "The only difference between the artist and the other fellow is that the artist, the genius, chooses to do his job freely without prostituting himself and without compromising himself. The other fellow, Mr. Average Man, prostitutes himself in a manner so that he may gain material profits. Profit and prostitutes, and eventually death, sleep in the same bed."

Benny, disillusioned and angry, left San Francisco and returned to Greenwich Village. On the train going back to New York he remembered his father's words: "You'll starve all your life if you follow this crazy idea of being an artist! You'll starve! Where you get this crazy idea? Nobody in my family is artist. My father was politician and I follow the great Garibaldi. Your mother, she is woman. She love you and she encourage you. But she not know the world. It is right that my son follow my teaching. Being an artist is not for boys in my family. Go out! Fight for freedom! Don't waste your time playing with plaster and mud. You are big boy now, not baby play with mud pies!"

And he remembered his answer: "Papa, I'll be the one that does the starving, so don't you mind!"

Bufano did not know that he would follow the teachings of both his mother and his father. The mud pies would become great statues of hard materials, and he, Bufano, would always be in the midst of a fight for peace and freedom.

In New York, Bufano did not go home but went directly to his studio in Greenwich Village, an old garage of the former Russian Institute in MacDougal Alley. It was a refuge where no contracts and no politicians could tell him what to do.

Bufano remembered how he had rented the studio, before he had gone to San Francisco. He had seen a "for rent" sign on the fly-specked window. He had pressed his nose close to the window and saw a tiny room with a dirt floor, rough unpainted wooden walls, dark with age and dust and with the studs showing. To young Beniamino these studs were like beautiful marble columns, and the shabby room was a jeweled sanctuary, a refuge and a promise of blessed solitude. The rent was twelve dollars a month. Bufano had gone to Jim Fraser, for whom he had been working, to tell him of his find. Fraser, remembering his own youth, knew what his first studio must mean to the young artist; he lent Bufano the first month's rent and gave him some tools. Bufano ran back to the Alley, paid the rent and entered his studio.

For a long moment he stood inside the door without moving. He couldn't believe it was his. His delighted eyes wandered about the dismal room and stopped at an object in the corner. An old iron stove! He grabbed some old newspapers piled high in a corner, stuffed them into the stove and put a match to them. The fire flared up and brought the room to life. But he needed to furnish the bare room with a few more essentials.

He walked to Abe's Second Hand Furniture Shop in the Village. Abe was a large, grizzled old man with a paunch, a gray beard and a wrinkled face with humorous dark eyes. He knew most of the artists of the village and had great respect for their work. He knew the poverty of the young ones and helped them when he could. Beniamino bought an ancient iron cot, rusted and dirty, and a sturdy bench, both for one dollar. As he started to leave, his eyes lit on a ragged Moroccan coverlet spread over a broken couch. He stopped to finger its rough-textured material. It had a beautiful primitive design of faded red roses on a dirty, white hand-loomed cloth. Abe threw it in for nothing. That evening Remo and Cesare, Beniamino's brothers, carried the bench and cot to the studio. Benny lugged his old mattress, and Lucrecia trailed behind them with the Moroccan spread.

Benny set up the bench while the boys cleaned the cot with an old rag. Lucrecia spread the cover over the cot, then stood back to view the effect. It was dirty. She was about to remove it from the cot when Beniamino stopped her. He didn't want it washed.

"This is my studio, Mama. And I don't care if it's dirty. I like the dirty white color." He tore the coverlet from her hands and put it back on the cot.

Lucrecia turned and stalked angrily out of the studio.

"You hurt Mama's feelings," Remo said.

"Well, I don't want Mama always telling me what to do. She can boss Papa around, but not me." Bufano was no longer the child wrapped in the shawl of his mother's love, but a young man and a genius, with a heart full of ideals, ready to face the world.

"You think you're a big guy now," said Cesare. "Gettin' too big for your britches! I'll take you down a peg." And Cesare gave Benny a hard punch in the chest.

"Cut it out you two," said Remo, pulling Cesare away. "Let's get to work."

As Beniamino returned the punch, Lucrecia entered. The fight stopped. Lucrecia sat down on the floor and told the boys to join her. "I'm going to tell you a story about peace," she said, "so you boys listen." It was typical of Lucrecia to tell stories whenever she had a problem to discuss, and the boys maintained a respectful silence. Having never learned to speak English, she told her story in Italian, her tired face alight.

"It was in the little village of Gubbio," she said, "that a wolf was plaguing the inhabitants by raiding their yards of fowl and lamb, and sometimes even killing the children.

"St. Francis called the wolf to him and said in a gentle reproving voice, 'Why do you plague the villagers and kill their fowl and their lambs and their children?'

"The wolf answered, 'I am hungry, O Holy Man. The villagers hate me. They throw stones and shoot arrows at me. They want to kill me. But I am more clever than they. I outsmart them. I hunt their animals and eat them. Sometimes, in the winter, I kill their children when I can find no other food to eat!'

" 'Why do you not eat me, Wolf? Why do you lie at my feet as gently as a newborn lamb?'

" 'You are not my enemy,' the wolf said simply, looking up at St. Francis with love in his eyes.

"Then St. Francis went to the villagers, the wolf trotting at his feet. Seeing the fright in the eyes of the people, St. Francis spoke, 'He will do you no harm. Let us solve your differences.'

"The people shouted, 'He has killed our animals and our children. We will kill him. We are at war with him!'

" 'War is not God's way,' St. Francis answered. 'The wolf was hungry and he stole your lambs because there was no food for him to eat. He killed the children because he knows no better. If you will put out food for him to eat, the wolf will promise not to molest you.'

"The people consulted with their mayor. Then the mayor asked St. Francis, 'Will you give us your word on that?'

"St. Francis looked down at the wolf. The wolf gave his promise. 'I will give you my word as surety,' St. Francis said. 'You can now be friends with the wolf.'

"The mayor came to the feet of St. Francis and knelt beside the wolf. St. Francis blessed them both. From that day forth the wolf came every day for his portion of food. The children played with the wolf and rode on his back. There was peace in the village of Gubbio."

"That's how I remember my mother telling this ancient story to us while we sat on the floor of my studio," Bufano said. "I think she told us the story to prove to us that peace was more humane than war, and I know she was right. What's the good of war? Where does it get anybody, killing off a bunch of innocent people? This was my mother's answer." Bufano never forgot the lesson. Peace became his obsession, St. Francis his ideal.

He remembered that shortly after Lucrecia left, Jim Fraser entered the studio carrying a chunk of marble. He had brought a present to inaugurate Bufano's new studio. Beniamino placed the piece of marble tenderly on the floor in the corner and told Fraser he'd be afraid to start chiseling on it. Fraser warned him not to be in a hurry and to wait for the right time. He explained there was a creature in that chunk of stone. Perhaps a cat. If the artist was patient, suddenly one day that cat would want to be born, and that was the minute to start chiseling. Bufano had learned an important lesson in sculpturing. Fraser wished him good luck and told him he would be a great artist someday.

Cesare had listened to all of this with a jaundiced expression. In effect he said to his brother," No wonder you think you're so great. You're nothing but a little snot-nose and don't you forget it! Come on, Remo, let's get the hell out of her and leave this genius do his great work."

Remo looked thoughtful, hoping he'd be an artist too someday. And later Remo did become a famous artist: he made some of the most beautiful puppets in the world.

Next morning Benny got a letter from Gertrude Vanderbilt Whitney, a very close friend of Fraser's. She would like to pay the rent of the studio so that he would be free to work without too much worry about expenses. Bufano didn't tell his father about this. He knew his father would consider it charity to allow a wealthy woman to pay his rent.

Again he looked at the chunk of marble. It did not speak to him. The image in the marble was not yet awakened. Bufano was inspired with the desire to do something small. Medallions! That was what he wanted to do. He became medallion-happy. Everything he looked at was transformed into a medallion: a picture of his father's former friend, the mayor of Rome; two dogs that roamed the streets of Greenwich Village; his drama teacher at the neighborhood house; Robert Paine's two children; a young artist friend with a pipe in his mouth; an older man with a beard; a picture of the twins, Romulus and Remus, being suckled by the wolf; and Paul Manship, the famous sculptor, as well as his wife.

Six months later he was sick of medallions. Now he was ready for something big. He opened a book to a picture of Michaelangelo's David: he would sculpture his own David. He worked for weeks on it. Finished, it was a ten-foot statue, modeled in clay then cast in an aggregate of cement, stone and other materials, called cast stone. It was an impressive David, with the powerful limbs and body of a fighter and the face of a leader of men. And a dreamer.

Bufano had worked at his statue passionately and without stopping, as though death were at his heels and would interrupt him before it was completed. Death was at the heels of the entire Western world, he thought. Europe was in World War I and Wilson was desperately trying to keep out of the conflict. Of this the young artist working in his studio was sure.

He looked at his David standing in one corner and at the board on which he had mounted his medallions. He felt proud of these works. They gave him the courage to go home now and face his father for the first time since his return from San Francisco.

2 ' The Immigrant in America

In the apartment, Canio and Lucrecia were making artificial flowers. This was piece work, brought home by Canio for all the family to work on. Lucrecia, as usual, greeted her son with a kiss on each cheek; Canio looked glum, as he always did when working on the flowers. He hated the work and was shamed that a man who had been a Garibaldine and someone of importance in San Fele, Italy, should have to stoop so low in the land of gold, milk and honey.

Canio wanted to know if Beniamino had made his fortune in California. Beniamino told them of his disappointment and sorrow over the way he'd been treated by the authorities of the exposition. Canio became furious and threw down his work, crushing some of the roses he was making. It was just as he'd expected. His son was a fool for wanting to be an artist and for letting himself be cheated by a bunch of exploiting robbers and crooks.

Lucrecia listened to the tirade, giving her son a sympathetic glance and laying her hand on his shoulder to pacify him. But Beniamino was not to be pacified. He was proud of having been selected by Manship to do the enlargements and reminded Canio that he now had his own studio and was an artist, accepted by the other great artists of the Village. Not only that, but Mrs. Gertrude Vanderbilt Whitney was his patron. To his own surprise, he even defended the San Francisco authorities by saying he didn't have a contract so it wasn't their fault.

Canio countered by telling him that if you're honest a contract didn't matter, and besides he had made a beggar out of himself by letting Mrs. Whitney pay his rent, which was the same as charity.

Beniamino resented this implication and screamed that it
wasn't charity, and that in Italy most great artists depended
upon a patron to help them. It wasn't charity! He hated charity!
"I'll tell you what charity really is," he told his father. "It's
accumulated injustice looking out at escaping convicts." Benny
himself didn't know exactly what he meant, but it was enough
to squelch his father.

Lucrecia tried to pacify the two but the hot Italian tempers
were too much for her. Beniamino ended up by banging out
of the apartment and going back to his studio.

He was about to settle down to his work when, in the mail,
he received a copy of *The Immigrant in America Review*. The
return address was Mrs. Whitney in Roslyn, New York. Mrs.
Whitney had suggested the idea of a contest to the editors of
the *Review*. She thought that an art contest could best develop
"the meaning of America to the immigrant and of the immigrant to America; America as a fusion of many races, traditions
and forces molded into a vital and unified whole; America as
the land of Freedom and of Opportunity for individual development and growth." Beniamino, the ever-ready, immediately decided to enter the contest, but he was not blindly accepting all
these high-sounding and noble ideas.

While thinking about the contest, he had a vivid memory
of the day he first met Mrs. Whitney, and the painful result of
that meeting. He recalled the day, almost two years before, that
he was working on a drawing of a buffalo, because Fraser had
been commissioned to design the buffalo nickel. Bufano realized that a woman was looking over his shoulder as he worked.
He heard her ask James Fraser if he would lend the young
artist to her for a while: she needed help on the group she
was sculpturing for the city of Washington, D.C. Fraser told
her it was up to Bufano; she must ask him.

She did ask him and the boy, although shy in the presence
of a woman of such wealth and importance, said at once that
he would be glad to work for her. Fraser told her she was for-
tunate because Bufano was the best clay puddler in the Alley.
Mrs. Whitney explained that the work would be done in her

studio in Roslyn and that Bufano would have to stay there until it was completed. Beniamino didn't care where he went as long as he was working.

She stopped to admire the group Fraser was making of her with her three daughters. After complimenting Fraser on the work, she told Beniamino that she would pick him up at Fraser's studio in the morning. He was to bring his clothes with him. After she left, Fraser told Beniamino that she was a wonderful woman but not a very happy one.

Beniamino could not understand how she could be so rich and still be unhappy; she certainly could buy anything she wanted.

Fraser explained that there were some things you can't buy. He hinted that perhaps her riches were a burden to her as an artist, since she could never be sure that praise was heaped upon her because of her fine art, and not merely because she was a Vanderbilt and a Whitney. The rich have their own particular problems, Fraser explained. Beniamino concluded that the problems of the rich were as nothing compared to those of the poor.

Fraser teased him about stepping into very high society, saying that he would be turning up his nose at the poor devils in MacDougal Alley after rubbing elbows with the high and mighty of Roslyn.

The following day Lucrecia packed Beniamino's few clothes in a paper shopping bag that was given out free when you bought enough groceries. She was proud of her son, telling Canio that Beniamino must be a good sculptor or Mrs. Whitney wouldn't ask for him to help her. She was a Vanderbilt, she reminded Canio.

Canio responded that the Vanderbilts were nothing but a bunch of exploiters.

Beniamino kissed his mother, picked up his bag and his violin and rushed over to meet Mrs. Whitney. He sat in the front seat with her in the small electric car, edging as close to the door as possible, not feeling comfortable until he arrived safely at her estate. In her studio was an enormous mural on one wall. Beniamino thought it looked a little like "a military thing" with all the people and horses in it. Mrs. Whitney explained that her sportsman husband loved horses and owned five hundred of them. That's why she had had this mural done. Beniamino sensed that horses were all he cared about.

Bufano admired the elegant marble-walled bathroom. With a wry smile Benny thought it wouldn't be bad to fall into this toilet. He was thinking of the group of privies in back of the tenement building at home on Sullivan Street, one privy with a two-holer per floor. He remembered the horrifying experience he had there in his earlier childhood, shortly after his family arrived in the United States. He had had a bad time adjusting his small rump to the hole, and while on the throne one day he slid in. He yowled and howled, crying for help. Half an hour later he was dragged out, a malodorous bit of humanity.

In the mirror of Mrs. Whitney's fancy bathroom Bufano saw himself: an adolescent boy, barely five feet tall, with small blue eyes, and a thin brown-skinned face, too old and too intense for his years. Scuffed worn shoes, the shoestrings broken and re-tied into knots, hugged the small feet. Short faded socks flopped uneasily over the shoes. The cotton corduroy pants, baggy at the knees, had fringed at the bottoms from too-long wearing. The faded blue shirt, blotched with gobs of clay, some buttons missing, the cloth worn threadbare, was pierced by thin, sharp, childish elbows. The bushy hair, too long uncut, straggled down onto the thin neck.

He looked for a long time at his image. He had never seen himself from head to toe this way. There were no full-length mirrors in his slum apartment. For the first time he was embarrassed by his shabby clothes, here in this elegant home. But I'm an artist, he thought, and artists don't have to be rich in money. I'm rich in my art and that's all that matters. Mrs. Whitney is an artist too, but she needs me to complete a job. If I had that job I wouldn't need her. Maybe that's why she's unhappy. He left the bathroom, his heart uplifted and a little proud.

Beniamino noticed the beauty of the place and its exquisite appointments, but he felt sorry for the servants who waited on the owners. Bufano was astonished at the amounts of food served, remembering his own family and how his mother used to sit before the big bowl of spaghetti with small bits of meat in it, spooning out meager portions. He remembered the bowl scraped clean at the end of the meal and the little twinge of hunger, unappeased, when he left the table. But he also remembered with nostalgia the large family always around the table, always laughing, talking, quarreling. Never in all the time he was at the Whitneys' did the entire family eat together.

He had often seen Mrs. Whitney at Fraser's studio but his shyness precluded his looking at her closely; now he noticed that Mrs. Whitney moved gracefully. Fraser had taught him to observe closely the movements of animals as well as humans and to notice how the human frame was articulated, how muscles moved as a person fell into various positions: sitting, walking, standing, leaning, bending, running or swinging an arm. It was becoming second nature for Benny to watch, observe and record in his memory what he saw. His drawings later showed this close observation, as do his sculptures.

In the studio Mrs. Whitney wore an old smock. Working at one side of the studio was a man of about fifty, whom Mrs. Whitney introduced as Andre, the expert at making armatures. These are the basic metal structures, done from sketches of the final sculpture, on which the clay model is moulded by the artist. Benny learned that the armature acts as a support for the clay just as the skeleton does for the bodies of humans and animals. Andre and the young artist became good friends.

Andre lived in a small pleasant room on the ground floor in back of the building. Bufano liked this kindly, gentle man. They worked together in the studio, and often in the evenings, when the family went to the big house, they spent time together. Usually Benny went to Andre's room to play duets; Andre played the flute and Bufano the violin. He had taken violin lessons from a spinster who earned a sparse living by teaching the potential virtuosi of Greenwich Village.

After the duets Andre would lead the way to the edge of the woods to feed the wild animals that lived on the estate. Beniamino would follow Andre out into the night and walk

across the acres of meadow. There, on the edge where the trees
became thick, in moonlight bright as day, they saw little animals eating. Woodchucks, raccoons and moles, all busily picking up the food Andre had scattered for them. Andre would
walk very slowly and carefully to the animals; he would stand
for a long time among them as they continued to eat, ignoring
him. Then, very slowly, he would lean down and pick up a mole.
For an instant it would squirm in his hand, but as Andre stroked
its soft fur with a gentle finger it quieted and nibbled at the
bread he held out to it. He would very carefully put it into
Benny's outstretched hand. It was unafraid. Bufano stroked it,
delighted at the smooth simplicity of its lineaments. The little
boy from Sullivan Street learned the ways of the wild creatures,
learned to love them and to model them. "We don't know if
animals are happy or not," he said, "but at least they're less
complicated than humans."

Puppy love had never entered Benny's life. He never went
to dances because he couldn't dance and never learned because
he was too shy. The only love he had for a woman, aside from
his deep love for his mother, had been for the nun, Antonia,
daughter of the wood carver Ranieri. Benny was no more than
eleven years old when Ranieri's wife asked him to deliver a
bundle of clothes she had collected for the nuns to give to the
poor. He went happily and returned starry-eyed; he told Ranieri
that he planned to marry Antonia because she was so beautiful.

"Nuns don't get married," Ranieri explained. "At least not
to mortals. They're the brides of Christ. Dedicated persons
should never get married. A great artist should never marry.
A woman holds a man back," was Ranieri's opinion. Bufano took
this advice seriously, as is evidenced in the fiasco of his marriage
years later. He continued to love Antonia even though he had
to give up his plans for marrying her. Gradually, throughout the
years, his love for Antonia merged with his love of Christ.

Although Beniamino's interest in Antonia was from afar, his
next interest in a girl was a little closer. At the Whitney's he
was thrown into the company of the Whitney daughters. In his
own words he "fell in love with Barbara." He watched her with

loving eyes, but when she approached him or talked to him he felt shy and afraid.

Throughout his adolescent years Lucrecia showed much concern about her Beniamino and his reluctance to be with girls. To Bufano, they not only took him away from his greatest love, art, but they were a luxury he couldn't afford. He also had little time for baseball, football, basketball, or other sports that most boys played at.

"You'll never get married," said Lucrecia, "if you don't go with girls."

Benny would just shrug his shoulders and change the subject.

When he was seventeen, Lucrecia was irritated with her son for another major lack in his interests — the Catholic church. She had brought him up, she thought, with the proper respect for people, for animals, and for the church. But its ritual and formalities were too much for him. Here the negative influence of his father, Canio, was much stronger, as Canio always denounced churchgoers as hypocrites. "Stay away from all churches," he used to say. And although Canio, in his own youth, had almost taken the vows of a priest, he claimed to his children that the pope and the church were the ruination of mankind. Canio always punctuated his condemnation of the church with, "I know what I'm talking about. You would too if you lived in Rome in my day."

Rome in my day! Canio had lived through hectic days in his time. It was hell, Canio would say, steaming up his sons to fever pitch when he told them of his revolutionary tactics as a Garibaldine. At that time King Humberto II was the scourge of Italy, said Canio, and with his warring, taxing, screwing, and hating he turned the people against him. When Humberto's armies were soundly trounced at Aduwa by African hordes, his goose was cooked; there were strikes, riots, and bombings all over the monarchy. Canio stuck out his chest, full of pride, as he told of his active part in the strife, which by 1900 finally resulted in a shot through the head for the king.

The king was dead, but with the furious search for the assassins no one's head was safe. Certainly not Canio's. Conspirators and their sympathizers left Italy in droves, but Canio had a serious problem that detained him — his beard. Canio had an impressive head, to hear Lucrecia tell the story, with a great beard flowing from his chin. "It was so beautiful," said Lucrecia wistfully. Canio agreed. But Canio had to leave the country or die. Only one solution: the beard must go, then no one could recognize him. Instead of his head, the beard came off one day, leaving his chin as hairless as the bottom of his son Beniamino, then two years old. Canio left his secret hiding place to see Lucrecia for the last time.

At home in San Fele, Lucrecia was sitting in an old rocker holding Beniamino. Lucrecia, her dark Italian eyes sparkling, told the rest of the story with dramatic flair: "The door opens slowly. A stranger enters. He sneaks in. Grins at me, this bum. I drop Beniamino into a basket full of clothes. I chase the intruder out with a broom. I pick up Beniamino again. All is well. Then, that man comes in again. He smiles, and then I know. It is Canio. Disguised. Without a beard. His beautiful beard. I cry, but I'm happy. Canio can now get away without losing his head!"

Canio and Lucrecia made plans to get Lucrecia and the children to the United States. Canio said he would get there somehow. The streets are paved with gold, said Canio, echoing the exaggerated platitude of the thousands who had preceded him. "The millionaires," he said, "swarm the sidewalks of New York like flies on a dung heap." Amid crying and kissing and last minute farewells, Canio slipped away, not to be heard from again for more than four months. He was in New York. He was making a fortune, he wrote, and soon would send enough money to bring them all over to New York.

His fortune didn't add up to enough until more than a year had passed. Lucrecia and the rest of the Bufanos finally arrived in New York on June 18, 1902. Although only four at the time, Beniamino could still recall the revolting horror of shipboard smells in the torments of seasickness, of being tossed about by the surging seas, of the terrifying moan of fog horns, of frightened emigrants praying to the Madonna to save them from a watery grave.

The ship was due. Canio had slept in Battery Park all night so he could be ready to greet his family the first thing in the morning at Castle Garden, the entry depot for immigrants. Red tape. Medical shots. Examinations. Inspections. And then, finally it was all over. The first thing Lucrecia saw was not Canio, but his beard, his lovely beard, and it was as stately as ever. In the excitement of the greetings, Beniamino accidentally hit his father on the nose. "Ah, a fighter," said Canio, predicting a characteristic of Benny's that many others would learn about firsthand in the years to come.

It was a shocking disappoinment to Lucrecia to find that Canio's "fortune" depended on making artificial flowers, a process so slow that if he earned twenty dollars a week it was miraculous. He must have lived only on chestnuts, thought Lucrecia, sadly reminded of the wonderful chestnuts they used to have in San Fele.

The tall buildings in New York at first surprised her, but the people and the stores were very much like home. It was predominantly an Italian neighborhood that they lived in, sprinkled here and there with some Jews and Irish. The people spoke Italian; even the signs in the shops were in Italian. One of Lucrecia's fears about moving to America was that she'd have to learn a new language to get along. Here, she didn't need to learn English at all, and without such motivation she never did learn the language of her adopted land.

The railroad apartment, where Canio took them to live upon their arrival, was at 143 Sullivan Street, near Washington Square in Greenwich Village. The older Bufanos thought that it would only be temporary quarters, but more than a half century later they would both die in the same flat. It was a typical apartment for New York: a long hall, like the aisle of a railroad coach, with a flickering gas jet giving off a ghastly blue light in the ceiling, and doors that led into the tiny rooms of the apartment. Inside, at one end was the living room and at the other the kitchen.

Sullivan Street and its slums set the groundwork for Beniamino's love of animals, mainly mice and cats, of which there were a great many in his neighborhood. Benny recalled that at ten he produced his first animal sculpture: "My first animal was a mouse. I had lots of practice watching them when they scampered around on the exposed water pipes in our bathroom and kitchen." It was at Ranieri's studio; Beniamino worked for an hour on a small piece of wood, wood that seemed to have a figure in it that wanted to be born. Slowly, he gouged and cut away the wood. The head was born first, then gradually the little animal was released and Beniamino held in his hand the newborn creature. Ranieri took it in his hand and turned it about, looking at it from all angles. "Good," he said. "A little rough here and there, but good." He patted Beniamino on his head. "My little Michelangelo," he said. "My little Michelangelo." Always the ten-year-old boy would remember that.

In addition to his not being a good Catholic, Lucrecia found still another fault in Beniamino. He, with a group of other Catholic boys, showed a growing interest in a settlement house affiliated with a Protestant church, of all things. The director, a Mr. Nardie, developed Beniamino and three other boys into a group called the Missionary Tramps. All the boys were talented leaders, singers, and talkers, so the group became proficient at proselytizing and was in great demand in outlying areas. But one day Benny became disillusioned. He heard two missionaries tell the congregation that Sunday is a day of rest, that to work then was a sin. Benny was thoughtful. Weren't the missionaries working on Sunday? And when he saw the same two men leave the church and drive away in a limousine driven by a chauffeur, that was too much. They shouldn't have left that poor chauffeur sitting out in the cold while they were in church. They should practice what they preached.

He remembered what Mr. Nardie had told him once: "You're a sculptor, Beniamino. You know that rotten wood cannot be carved. You've got to be good all the way through. That's the way of the good Christian." Bufano believed that. He would give up the Missionary Tramps and have nothing more to do with the City Missions. His prejudice against missionaries in the years to come, particularly in China, would dominate his thoughts about Christianity.

He was learning different sorts of things at Mrs. Whitney's. His knowledge about the psychology of people was beginning to crystallize. As a boy from a slum area with poverty-stricken parents he knew about poor people and how they behaved. Now, he was observing firsthand how the rich behaved. He saw Mrs. Whitney as an intense, driving woman. Since she had obtained her commission to work on a big art project, her whole life centered about getting the work done as soon as possible. She handed Bufano some sketches and told him to model these in plasticine. At first, he was careful to follow the sketches, but soon he substituted his own creative work. For some time Mrs. Whitney watched him, saying nothing, then suddenly she became angry and told him to keep to the sketches. Bufano could not, would not follow her sketches. He was always an individualist; he was not a copier but a creative artist. He looked scornfully at the sketches Gertrude Whitney had made. He couldn't copy slavishly what someone else had designed. His fingers responded to his own talent and there was no curbing them. Mrs. Whitney continued to reprimand him for taking liberties with her sketches. He paid no attention and went merrily on his own way. One day the whole thing blew up: Mrs. Whitney smashed his models!

Seeing his work broken on the floor was a shattering experience to the fifteen-year-old boy. Speechless with horror, he dashed to his room, packed his few possessions in the shopping bag and ran through the estate grounds to the road. There he hitched a ride to New York and to Fraser. Fraser listened, scratched his head, and put him back to work. Bufano returned to his studio-home; Mrs. Whitney had promised to pay the rent and she kept her promise.

After recalling these past experiences with her, Benny reread the article in the *Review*, "The Meaning of America to the Immigrant." He remembered Ranieri telling him that in preparing for a job, it took ninety percent preparation to ten percent execution if he wanted the job done well. Ranieri had made him work on small scraps of wood before giving him a large piece.

Disillusionment vanished in his preparation for the sculpture to be submitted to the *Immigrant in America* contest. His work, he told Mrs. Whitney one day, might not please Americans but it would tell the truth.

She replied that he had a right to tell the truth as long as he wasn't bitter.

Benny wouldn't be bitter but he couldn't be sweet either. He had to tell the truth in his own way.

For three months he studied the truth. To him, the swarms of Jewish immigrants on Hester Street, at their pushcarts, barking out their wares, were the truth. The dispossessed families sitting out on the sidewalk with their furniture, like junk, piled around them. That was truth. The horror of eviction, the menace of the landlords, the haggling of the people for every hard-earned penny were the truth. The degrading names the immigrants were called . . . wop . . . sheeny . . . mick . . . nigger . . . frog . . . slant-eye . . . chink . . . dago. These were the truth. So also was the dismal railroad apartment, where he had lived for fifteen years with his family of seventeen crowded into it, the truth. His weeks of hard work at the exposition and the answer he got when he asked to be paid for his own creative works. These, too, were the truth.

He remembered Lucrecia sitting on the floor of his studio telling the story of St. Francis and the Wolf. To Benny, truth was peace. It was neither of creed nor race. It was not of the street; it was not of the temple. It was neither of darkness nor of light. It was an extension of the soul of man in his adventure beyond reality.

Many were the arguments with his friends. They called him a damned fool and told him he'd never win the contest. Benny yelled that he was just telling the truth. Who wanted to know the truth, his friends asked sarcastically; art and propaganda weren't related. It wasn't propaganda, Bufano maintained. Every work of art must have inner meaning. If there's no thoughtfulness or meaning, there was just emptiness and decoration, not art.

"I came unto my own and my own received me not." Bufano inscribed this Biblical quotation at the base of a many-figured group which he submitted to the contest.

In December of 1915 Bufano was notified, to his amazement, that he had won the first prize of $500. In the *Outlook* of December 15th of that year the following article read in part:

> Beniamino Bufano, "one of the Bufano boys," as his neighborhood calls him, "Benny" to the artist folk for whom he worked, has won the $500 prize for the best sculpture submitted in the contest inaugurated last summer by the *Immigrant in America Review*.

> That the greatest prize went to an Italian, almost a boy, one of fifteen brothers and sisters, himself an immigrant . . . is truly dramatic, but it is Bufano's interpretation of the contest which quickens curiosity. He says stoutly that he "did not try to please Americans but to tell the truth."

> Bufano has proved, by his own history that opportunity yet waits at the door of young America, but he has made of his work an indictment of those who despise the alien and exploit him. There are more than thirty figures in it, oppressed peoples who seek the promised land, and, finding it, find oppression there. At their head he has put a sturdy youngster in defiant pose, as if in challenge to a prejudice which ranks all aliens as "Dagoes," "Chinks," "Niggers," or at its mildest, "Those ignorant foreigners."

This write-up is the last vestige Bufano had of this work: the sculpture was later destroyed. But Bufano had sought the truth, studied it, created it and won the prize with it.

Beniamino raced down to the office of the *Review*, where he picked up his check for $500, then ran home excitedly and waved it before the family. This, too, was the truth! Lucrecia turned to her husband triumphantly and told him that some day her son would be a rich man as well as famous.

Canio took the check from Beniamino and turned it over suspiciously in his hand. "Hm," he said. "Five hundred dollars. I betcha they cheated you. Some guy higher up is raking in a lot of graft out of this."

3 ⟋ The Martyr for Peace

For the first time Bufano felt that he belonged in America and to America. He felt that his adopted land was now really his, that the people were his people and that he was theirs. Here, with these people, in his land, lay the hope of the future. If the world was ever to have a lasting peace, then his fellow Americans would be the ones to originate it; these were the people he could depend upon to help carry out his ideals. And as a young man just turned eighteen, he was developing a strong messianic conviction that he would be the one to help create a lasting peace in this world. He was getting ready to assume his important role as a leader of peace through art. The American people had a great man to lead them, a former university president, a great lover of peace and freedom, and this man, President Wilson, would keep the peace and never let this country get entangled in war. Bufano was sure of it. He would bet his life on it.

Beniamino was now on Easy Street with his fortune in his pocket. He swaggered a bit before the friends who had predicted a failure. He who has, gets, say the sidewalk philosophers, and Benny was no exception. Mrs. Whitney, his patron, rented for him a larger studio, a remodeled stable in Washington Mews.

One day Lucrecia dropped in to see Benny in his studio. She liked to sit and watch her son at his work. She saw that he was troubled but she said nothing, just sat down, her hands folded in her lap. He was modeling a small nude figure of a man in clay. She told Beniamino that she liked to watch his hands — they were so sure in their work. She asked what he was modeling. He explained that it was the Christ, the Man of sorrow — the

Christ sorrowing for His children, the young boys who were dying on the battle fields. Bufano once said he remembered how she raised her eyes to Heaven and prayed that her children would never have to go to war.

Watching her he felt he must model a portrait of her and asked her to pose for him. Lucrecia was flattered and came the following afternoon as she promised. Sometimes, weary from her hard work, she would fall asleep. At these times he studied carefully the deep lines — formed by a life of hardship, poverty, childbearing and sorrow — the dark hair smoothed over the wrinkled forehead, the wide mouth, strong yet gentle and understanding.

The finished portrait was in blue and green stone terra cotta. Years later at the Paris exhibition of October, 1927, Roger Fry, the great English art critic, said about this portrait: "A simple rendition of sculptural form in portraiture. Here, Bufano betrays himself as an Italian; a lover of simple beauty. A sensitive and plastic poem of old age and youth, all in one."

"My mother," said Bufano, "always fell asleep when she posed for me. That always pleased me. She would come to my studio every day in the afternoon to take a nap. While she slept I would work on it and she never saw the portrait until I had finished with it. When she saw it for the first time she exclaimed, 'Oh my God! Do I look like that?' Later she used to say to me, 'My boy, you have a gift in your hands. If I were a sculptor, I would not make portraits of people. Look how much more beautiful and graceful the animals are and how much more grateful.'"

The portrait of his mother completed, Benny went back to his *Man of Sorrow*. He did the nude figure of Christ in cast stone, the arms folded, the head in profile as though turning away from war, from the tragedies of man. A pattern seemed to be developing in Benny's work. As he looked back upon it, it was easy to see. His later adolescent work seemed to be searching, crying out for an answer to his burning questions: Will man ever learn from his mistakes? Must Christ continually be crucified? What is the best way to depict the Truth in this world?

He never stopped working or learning. When he had time he studied with William Zorach, a sculptor who was developing a great reputation. Work — study — work — study. Little sleep, no recreation. He ploughed on as if he had but moments to live. On, on, on with truth and the love of mankind. He read every book he could find about peace, every book about the lives of great men, past and present. Surely, the answers must lie somewhere. He had no time to lose. On, on, on! Work! Work! His inner voice cried out to him always; when he wasn't working he felt guilty.

Beniamino was beginning to think things out. Through the maze of differing opinions on art, he winnowed out some thoughts of his own, some of them as abstract and abstruse as man can be:

> The abstract is abandoned realism. As long as you can conceive an idea that becomes an object and that you can talk about it, it ceases to be an abstraction. This means that the abstract and the real are one and the same in the process of thinking and doing. The abstract is thinkable only with the dead.
>
> A space, a line, a dot, realized in any given space is a picture, complete or incomplete, in all its realism.
>
> A good picture is married space, occupied as one unit of space of the object, and the space surrounding the object is known as empty space. A bad picture is unmarried space.
>
> Beauty can transform itself into any shape, form or sound, relative to its own law and existence. It pays no tribute to what is supposed to be real or to what is supposed to be abstract. The abstract and the real are provincial, human conveniences on a geographical level which are shortlived and mentally diseased.

Benny had brought home with him from San Francisco a clay head of Robert Paine's week-old baby. The infant was modeled with its eyes closed; the round baby face framed by a scalloped cap. Bufano was carving the head from a large block of wood. It was April 6, 1917. The peacefulness of the baby's face absorbed him and made him forget the horror of war hanging over the United States.

Benny always told the story of that fateful day as follows: suddenly the quiet of his studio was broken by the wild shouting of newsboys; he dropped his carving tool, ran out and bought a paper. The headlines screamed it: "*WAR!*"

Wilson had betrayed him!

Benny felt he had to protest, and the protest would be so horrifying, so powerful that the whole nation would rise up against the betrayer Wilson. He, Benny Bufano, would become the martyr for Peace. He would kill himself and leave a note saying that he did it in protest against war!

Then an idea that had made him shudder on the train to New York came back to him. Benny said he ran out of his studio and down the streets to his mother's apartment. No one was at home. He went into the kitchen, wrapped a meat cleaver in a piece of newspaper and raced back to the studio. He held the cleaver in his left hand, shuddering at what he was about to do. He would send it to Wilson! His trigger finger. He would send it to him in protest.

He lifted the cleaver and came down hard. There was no pain at first. His right hand spurted blood and two joints of his forefinger hung by a bit of flesh. He grabbed a towel, wrapped his hand in it, then ran down the street to Dr. Tomasulo, the family doctor. When he unwrapped his hand the doctor gasped. "Cut it off, quick!" Benny had said, then fainted dead away.

Dr. Tomasulo trimmed off the two joints and dressed the wound. Beniamino insisted on taking the severed part of his finger. He told the doctor he would send it to Wilson as "my contribution to the war effort."

The doctor told him he was crazy, that he was a green kid and took everything too seriously.

Bufano didn't care what the doctor said. He had to protest against going into war! He hated war more than anything in the world. He would fight against it all his life! He left the office and went back to his studio. He wrapped the piece of finger in cotton, put it in a box, enclosed a letter to Wilson explaining why he was sending it to him, and mailed it.

Bufano watched the papers every day expecting to see big headlines: "Boy chops off trigger finger and sends it to president as protest against war!" Nothing happened. No headlines. No letter from the White House. Soldiers were marching off to war. Thousands of young boys would die. He had made his sacrifice in vain.

Lucrecia had noticed that Benny's hand was bandaged. To a woman with fifteen children, a bandaged hand was no unusual sight. One evening she asked Beniamino why he was hiding his hand. He said it was "nothing." Benny had persuaded the doctor not to tell the family about the finger.

Canio wanted to know. "What do you mean by nothing?" What had he done? Maybe he cut it bad with the damn chisel. He was always chiseling away at that damn sculpture.

Benny did not answer.

Lucrecia asked suspiciously, "What did you do?" Maybe he had blood poison or something. Tomorrow he would go with her to Dr. Tomasulo!

Trapped, Benny told them what he had done, and his mother stared at him speechlessly. "The Bible said, 'If anything offend you, cut it off.' I don't want to use a gun. I don't want to kill people. I don't believe in war. I believe in peace. If I kept my trigger finger it would offend me."

4 ꞌ California and Canton

Benny returned to his studio to complete his work on the child of a wealthy Mrs. Rumsey whom he had met through Jim Fraser. When she came to his studio, he told her what he had done, saying he hoped his martyred trigger finger would be a lesson to warmongers. She was horrified at the thought of a human being chopping off his finger and told him that was worse than war. Discouraged and disappointed, Bufano said he was thinking of leaving for California as soon as the portrait of her baby was completed.

She paid him $2000 for the finished portrait and also financed his trip to Los Angeles. New York, the city of the immigrants' hope, had disillusioned him; in California he would pioneer his ideas through his art. From now on everything he did would speak of peace and the dignity of man.

California! Oranges and figs, palm trees and the lotus eater, land of sunny skies (no smog in 1917), a chamber of commerce dream! Benny, the child of sidewalks and asphalt, dreamed of living in an orange grove where he could pick the golden fruit right off the trees or sit high on the heavy limb of a fig tree, shut his eyes and put out a hand to pick a large, sweet, meaty blue fig and pop it into his mouth, skin and all.

Benny looked up the Russian sculptor, Prince Paul Troubetzkoy, soon after arriving in Los Angeles. Troubetzkoy, the son of a Russian nobleman and an American woman, was, like Bufano, born in Italy. The Prince had worked in Russia, France and Italy and now made his home in Los Angeles. Benny told Troubetzkoy that he was looking for a studio. The specifications were simple: cheap rent with some orange and fig trees near it.

Troubetzkoy laughed heartily. He had a place right in the middle of an orange grove. He wasn't sure about the fig tree, but he had never heard of a Southern California garden without a fig tree. It was his old studio in Pasadena, just an old shack, but Benny could have all the oranges he wanted to eat, and maybe he'd need them. The rent would be cheap; Troubetzkoy had never heard of a sculptor making any money at his art.

Bufano got the address, took the shopping bag in which he carried all of his worldly goods and promptly boarded a street car to Pasadena. The location was unequivocably the wrong side of the tracks, a neighborhood with a mixed population, but the old, neglected orange grove was, to him, a paradise. He immediately picked some oranges and ate them on the spot. Back of the orange grove he stopped in wonder. Fig trees, peaches, apricots, grapefruit — he was sure that he would never leave this paradise! Intrigued by the oriental design of the house next door, he wandered into the garden. Benny was greeted by a distinguished-looking Chinese gentleman who introduced himself as Dr. Wang.

Benny told him he was a sculptor, and he and Dr. Wang became close friends. They spent many hours talking about China, its philosophy and poetry, its culture and its political situation. Many evenings Dr. Wang would stroll over to drink white wine with lemon, Benny's favorite tippling.

Dr. Wang had a great respect for artists and loved to talk to Bufano. To Dr. Wang, the artist was the means through which beauty crystallized. They talked of critics and criticism and Dr. Wang, who had a large collection of fine recordings of the great composers, was furious at the invectives thrown at them in the past and the cruel discouragement of young artists. He expressed himself well and Bufano, always open to learning, wrote down what was said and later used these notes in lectures and writings.

Dr. Wang believed: "The savage ephemeral criticism of the contemporary critic arises out of a soul-blindness which prevents his achieving any universality of thought or feeling. This criticism, however, should not affect the artist negatively. The true artist can understand criticism, but not necessarily agree with it. He should observe the characteristic forms of nature, harken to his own imagination and creativity, and express his art in his life as well as in his chosen medium, approaching his work with a pure heart and an open mind."

Beniamino's response to this was: "A true artist lives for his art, which he loves for itself, not as a means of securing fleeting earthly pleasures or fame. The artist is only the means through which beauty is crystallized. I am convinced of the Taoist precept that genius lives in all mortal men, but that the artist is the one primarily alert to the impulse toward genius. Anything the true artist creates must be beautiful because anything other than beauty has become alien to him. Hence, for the artist, the one law is that there shall be no law, only the simplicity and purity which admits of spontaneous creation because it cannot help itself."

One evening Dr. Wang introduced a Chinese friend, Chung To, a cameraman for the Fox Film Company. Chung was impressed by Bufano's work, telling him that some day he would be famous. Benny said that he was already famous, that he had won a big contest. Chung, kidding him, asked if it was a beauty contest.

Chung drove Bufano around Hollywood. Benny was excited about the studios, the sets, the directors and the actors. The very artificiality of everything was so frankly and honestly exposed that Bufano found it a delight; he walked behind the sets and observed the beautiful architectural structures of supporting beams and cross beams. Chung introduced him to the movie world with its glamour and its colorful characters. Among these was Sid Grauman, who was then building the Chinese Theater. Grauman took to Bufano and visited his studio many times, watching him do a head of Dr. Wang in stoneware. When Grauman saw this beautiful piece of sculpture he asked Benny to make a portrait of himself. Benny completed it in a few months, and Grauman was so pleased that he paid $100 for it.

Bufano's life was well filled with work and study. Some evenings he took philosophy courses at the junior college in Pasadena. When he came home from his class, he and Dr. Wang often talked into the small hours about China. Dr. Wang knew many people who were personally acquainted with Sun Yat-sen, who was then battling for leadership of China. Dr. Sun was fighting to get better working conditions for the people of China.

San Francisco, sitting like a beautiful woman dressed in filth and rags under her splendid silken robes, looking out with far-seeing eyes over the sea to the mysteries, excitements and beauties of the Orient, beckoned to Bufano. Although still smarting 'from his treatment by the officials of the 1915 exposition, he had fallen in love with the city itself. He packed his belongings into a new shopping bag, gave the bust of Dr. Wang to the doctor, said good-bye to Chung To and took a bus to San Francisco, which would be his home for the rest of his life.

Upon arriving he went directly to Ying Choy and his wife, the young Chinese friends to whom he had given the *Honeymoon Couple*. They took him to their small apartment in China-town, then went out to find a studio for him. An old loft on the second floor of an ancient building on the corner of Sacramento Street and Grant Avenue satisfied his needs.

Two years had passed since he had won the five hundred dollars in the Whitney contest; the few coins left in Benny's pocket jingled dismally. Always welcome to eat with his many Chinese neighbors, he learned that some families ate at four o'clock, some at six. When the meal started a red curtain was traditionally hung at the door; it would be impolite to enter after the red curtain went up. Benny always managed to get there just before "red curtain time."

In his new studio Benny worked hard on a bas relief to be cast in bronze, *The First and Last Christians Who Died on the Cross*. This was to be a different interpretation from the usual crucifixion. Later, in the art journal *International Studio* an article stated that this was a young Christ on the cross,

> but not hung by the cruel spikes. He is suspended almost without weight, rising by His own spiritual exaltation, comes not within the compass of earthly things, though He is God's Son in the flesh, but is slightly disengaged with a detachment that at once expresses

his transcendence of corporeality and also creates the aesthetic isolation from the world of Natural things which is so difficult and so important in sculpture. And He is a young Christ not only because Jesus Himself was young, but because He was the voice of unsmirched youth in the world. "Suffer the little children to come unto Me and forbid them not; for of such is the kingdom of Heaven." And there are the little children, lovely solemn children in a row at the base of the cross. And all about the cross are fruit blossoms and singing birds, the springtime of the year and the renewal of life. All this, moreover, is in color, colored bronze in the one instance, stained red and copper-green and touched with gold, and colored glass in the example that is shown in the Arden Studios in New York, the colors of spring and new life.

The war had ended, but to Benny, the children at the feet of the Christ presented the young boys being sacrificed to the evil god of war, innocent Christlike victims, crucified. Is it significant that the forefinger of the right hand of the Christ is cut off at the second joint, as is Bufano's? Had Bufano identified himself and the phantom pains of his lost finger with Christ and His sufferings?

After finishing the Crucifixion, Benny started work on a fountain, *Children in the Rain*. When completed, the three-foot-high group was of two children, their arms about each other, their smiling faces wet with the rain, their hair in wet strands, streaming down over their foreheads. Roger Fry, the English critic, remarked about *Children:*

> Here he is at his best. Portraitures of glazed stone terra cottas . . . if they can be called portraits . . . because of the freedom that he takes with them. This very human side of him betrays his gentleness and tenderness . . . a simplicity that is only found in children.

While Bufano was working on the fountain, Ying Choy took him to meet Colonel Charles Erskine Scott Wood, an attorney who had recently moved from Portland to Los Gatos, California. Wood had been a distinguished and picturesque figure in the Northwest, but had given up the law to devote himself entirely to writing. As poet, essayist, and satirist, Wood was once described by a friend as "wise and mellow with many years . . . one who walks the fine-draped hills of Los Gatos with the Gods."

In Portland Wood had maintained two offices: one in which he met corporation clients; and another, a secret chamber to which came poets and artists, hobos, dreamers, borrowers, cranks, fanatics and gentle souls, sinners and saints and scientists. Benny was all of these to Wood except hobo and scientist.

Colonel Wood — "The Old Gentleman," Benny's favorite title for him — was just over seventy years of age when the two met. Wood wore a handsome gray tweed which set off his unruly shock of white hair and snowy beard and mustache. "You only noticed that he had a mustache when he opened his mouth. Otherwise, the mustache and beard looked like a great white muff stuck on under his nose to help hide his tie and collar." Bufano's first impression was that here was Moses or some dominant Biblical character. Wood's deep-set eyes gave him the appearance of severity, but the eyes themselves were kindly and receptive. Bufano liked him immediately.

He and The Old Gentleman became close friends. Their philosophies about people and the world were very much alike, and they shared almost the same point of view about war. Wood had written many short satires for *The Masses* magazine, but after the First World War his satires, dealing mostly with the war, became "untimely" and undesirable. The Old Gentleman said there would be no more war if the Golden Rule were believed and lived. Bufano agreed with this but wanted to know what other great thinkers felt and what philosophies they had evolved.

Always driven by his eagerness for education, Benny enrolled in classes at the University of California in Berkeley. He audited courses in poetry with Witter Bynner and in philosophy with John Dewey. While lecturing at the University, Dewey lived on Russian Hill in San Francisco. He knew Chinatown intimately, with all its alleys and dives, and introduced Benny to them and to his favorite Chinese restaurants. In the years that followed, Bufano and Dewey were to develop a close friendship. "Dewey even became my Godfather," Benny said. They were to share many experiences in their travels in the Orient. Over the years Dewey accepted Bufano's idealism and bemoaned the fact that the newspapers exploited him.

Bufano had completed the fountain of the *Children in the Rain* in jade stoneware when Chung To, the cameraman from Hollywood, moved in with him for a brief stay. The Fox Film Corporation had provided Chung with 12,000 feet of film for a trip to China to take newsreel movies of the temples, street scenes and people. Fox promised to pay $1.50 for each foot of film they accepted. Bufano, fired by the prospect of such a trip, asked Chung to take him along. Chung said okay, but who would pay for it?

Benny knew just the man. Within a week he had convinced Colonel Wood to finance his trip to China, but the next day Bufano received a letter from his brother Remo in New York:

Dear Brother:

Please come home right away. We are having trouble with Mama. She thinks you are arrested or maybe dead. She won't believe the letters you send are written by you. She thinks we are fooling her and writing the letters ourselves. So, please come home right away. Mama is crying.

Your brother
Remo

It was decided that Chung To would go on to China and that Benny would meet him later.

In June, 1918, an excited bushy-haired boy of twenty tumbled up the gangway of a ship about to leave for China. "He had no wardrobe, no hat, no coat, not even a toothbrush," wrote Witter Bynner, the poet, in a letter to one of the authors, describing Benny's last-minute boarding for the voyage. With the money from Colonel Wood, Benny had bought steerage passage, but he managed to wiggle his way up to first class. He did not know that his friend Bynner was on board. Bynner continued:

I had no idea that he was, as he said "penniless" at the time, thinking that his condition related merely to a characteristic and delightful recklessness. We went about among the passengers and made a collection of needed articles for him, even to the toothbrush.

It was to be a three-week voyage and Bufano was not one to waste three weeks away from his work. "He undertook to make a bust of me," wrote Bynner:

Somewhere I have a number of small snapshots of Benny, myself
and the bust, taken while he was working at it on the steerage
deck very near the prow, where he was certain we should be less
bothered by onlookers than elsewhere. Onlookers gathered but as
he foresaw, were not of a disturbing sort.

The bust was finished in plasticine before we reached Shanghai
where Benny wanted to cast and leave it until he should return
later and rejoin us. The Fickes [Bynner's travel companions] and I
were spending the summer at Mohanshan not far from Shanghai;
and Benny, though continuing on the steamer to Hong Kong where
he was to track down Chinese glazes, planned a reasonably speedy
return North.

Incidentally, the reason it had not occurred to me that he was hard
up was because he had told me that his quest for glazes was
being financed by Colonel Wood. I shall never forget our landing
at Shanghai and the mad episode of the casting. It was on a Sunday and the boat was to stay only a few hours. Not a place where
plaster might have been obtained, was open; so Benny ingeniously
telephoned an American doctor who, surprised but helpful, opened
his office and handed over his total supply of dental plaster to the
sculptor. A considerable period had passed before we reached this
point and sailing time was near. You should have seen Benny in
a fine frenzy scooping up handfuls of the wet plaster and flinging
them at my other head with the verve and force and dexterity of a
baseball pitcher. When the whole surface was covered he left the
ungainly object with me and dashed for the ship. It happened that
I was staying at a big Chinese hotel where the servants had the
head carefully boxed for me; but it also happened that Benny had
not returned to Shanghai when I left there a week or two later;
so I asked the management to store the box for me, carefully
labeled with my name.

I cannot now remember what happened to him during the suc-
ceeding months, but doubtless Benny can. I do remember that he
did not turn up again and that we did not meet, although I remained in Mohanshan into the autumn, our arrival at Shanghai
having been in early July. When it came time for me to sail home
I left the box with the hotel people, instructing them to deliver it
to Bufano who had written, I believe, from Hong Kong that some
time or other he would call for it. He can tell you what happened
next, how he called for it and how the hotel people refused to deliver it to anyone but me. Three years later I went again to Shanghai and inquired for my head! By that time all trace of it was lost
and I have had dreams of it set ludicrously alongside the foreign
visage of Marco Polo inside some Chinese temple. In any event, it
is lost to the western world.

While the head was resting peacefully in the big hotel at Mohanshan, Benny's life was anything but peaceful. The young exponent of peace had become embroiled in war!

In Hong Kong Benny had joined his friend Chung To, the cameraman. At this time the English controlled the customhouse in Hong Kong as well as the one in Canton. They were charging the Chinese double customs duty — first when the merchandise went through Hong Kong, then again at Canton. Bufano wanted to go to Canton and take pictures of the revolution, but Chung To wanted nothing of revolution; he didn't care who controlled the customhouse in Canton. Bufano pointed out that they could "make a fortune out of the pictures." Chung To wasn't sticking his neck into a revolution even if it meant a million dollars. He'd be alive and poor. Bufano was determined to go, so Chung To hid his camera and the film where Bufano couldn't find it.

Bufano "hung around" Hong Kong for two more weeks then went off to Canton alone. He made a bargain with the owner of a junk in the harbor to work for his passage up the Pearl River to Canton. He donned the coolie coat which he bought in the market for a few yen and helped load the junk with goods. The voyage up the river was slow. The junk had been in the family of its owner for many generations, and many years before they had stopped patching the ancient sails, so that now there were more holes than cloth. Bufano looked at them, wondering how they caught any wind to move the boat. The owner, his wife, five children and an old grandmother all lived on the junk. The grandmother lay in the bottom of the boat, never moving, her face leprous and her hands hideously distorted. The children fed her, but Benny, shocked, took over this chore; he couldn't stand seeing those kids exposed to leprosy. Somehow or other he felt immune.

At Canton he walked around the harbor, attracting no attention since he was in coolie clothes. He was sitting on a wharf, his feet dangling over the water, when "suddenly all hell broke loose." Guns spat fire, bullets zinged, men ran. Bufano jumped to his feet and ran with them. When the shooting stopped and the men sat down to rest, he found he had joined the revolution.

The traditional daily bowl of rice, occasionally laced with a fish head received from the soldiers, was welcomed by his hungry stomach, and sleeping on the ground or the hard planks of the harbor suited him just fine. He wandered the streets studying the ivory, jade and ebony carvings in the shops and admiring the gold work, lacquer and porcelain wares for which Canton was famous. He strayed into the back streets where he watched the women weaving, embroidering and making laces. Bufano didn't follow the revolution since he was too busy looking and learning.

The revolution in which Benny had found himself was an offshoot of the major uprising for which Sun Yat-sen was preparing. Benny, who had been belligerent and misunderstanding of his father's revolutionary activities in Italy, now found himself following in his father's footsteps. Benny excused his warlike tendencies on the basis that he was fighting injustice and that sometimes "you have to fight to achieve peace." But he did not bear arms and never injured an adversary; he was a "helpful Henry" to the revolutionists, and for his contribution he was learning firsthand about Taoism and the Chinese principles of pottery making.

He was particularly interested in porcelain ware. He went to Shekwan, a city a few miles west of Canton in the province of Kwantung, famous for its potteries. He learned that some of the Shekwan stoneware, mottled with blues, greys, browns, reds and greens, dated back to the Ming period. To learn their techniques in modeling and glazing, he joined a group of coolie potters and worked for his one bowl of rice a day.

In learning to understand the Cantonese people and their language he discovered that true Chinese decoration is never meaningless. Some symbols suggest good wishes, such as the peach, the crane, and the tortoise; the pine is for life, the bat for happiness, and the pomegranate for fertility. All the designs involved a deep study of the Chinese religion, history and folklore.

Later, Bufano brought home one of the most valuable collections of Chinese art then to be found in the West. The paintings, from the Sung and Ming periods, of flower studies and portraits contained pieces of extraordinary beauty. Though stained and faded a little by time, there was in them a beauty of color and design, a delicacy and sweep of rhythmic feeling hardly to be paralleled in Western art.

For the next two years he studied and labored hard with the potters. At night Benny was indistinguishable from the other coolies as he walked down the filthy, narrow streets with their hordes of children, pigs and chickens, their open sewers, their poverty and disease. He slept on a mat on the floor in a corner of the potters' shed; hunger and poverty were his constant companions. Bufano tightened his belt to ease the pangs and went on learning.

5 ⸴ Sun Yat-sen and Gandhi

Having absorbed all that the potters of Shekwan could teach him, Bufano wandered back to Canton. He roamed aimlessly about the city and became friendly with a band of Buddhist priests who slept in the streets and begged each morning for their one meal. They shared their meager food with him. By their example he learned the true meaning of charity and religion.

The priests were opposed to the work of the missionaries in China, claiming that they concentrated their attention upon the wealthy Chinese and neglected the coolie class. Some priests thought the missionaries weren't following the principles of a true religion and shouldn't be in China at all. Whatever the reason, Bufano wrote an article called "Does Anybody Care?" It was an indictment of the missionaries and their apparent blindness to the miseries of the poor.

He took the article to a Mr. Lee, editor of the *Canton Christian Times,* an English and Chinese periodical. Mr. Lee read it and said he couldn't possibly print it because it was libelous. Bufano argued violently. Mr. Lee compromised. Bufano would have to write the article as if it were a letter to the publication and sign it with his own name. Bufano agreed to this and the letter was printed.* A few days later he was called into the editor's office. Mr. Lee told him that Sun Yat-sen had read the letter and wanted to see him.

Sun Yat-sen, the physician and humanitarian, was about sixty years old. He was born of a peasant family in Chungshan and knew the hardships of the peasant classes. Although he had

---

*There is no available copy of this letter.

studied medicine at the University of Hong Kong and practiced in Macao, he had spent most of his life plotting against the Manchus. He had helped in the overthrow of the Manchu dynasty and aided in the establishment of the Chinese Republic. He was more a dreamer and idealist than a politician, and devoted his life to the betterment of the Chinese people. Bufano had learned this from reading and talking to the people in China. Benny presented himself to Dr. Sun, who surveyed the young man carefully then extended his hand in a friendly gesture toward a seat.

"So you are the author of 'Does Anybody Care?'" said Dr. Sun.

"Yes, I am." Dr. Sun introduced Bufano to others in the room — to Madam Sun Yat-sen and to a Chinese officer named Chiang Kai-shek.

"Weren't you afraid to sign your name to this letter?" the doctor asked.

"Why should I be afraid? I was telling the truth."

"Tell me more about this article you wrote. You must have questioned a good many people to write so feelingly about things foreigners ordinarily wouldn't know."

"It was not necessary to question people. You see, I've lived as a native of China for almost two years and have learned things firsthand, so everything I said in the paper was authentic and part of my own experience."

Bufano made such a favorable impression on Dr. and Madam Sun that they invited him to stay at their hilltop home in Canton. During that visit, Dr. Sun mentioned that he would appreciate it very much if Bufano could do something to help Americans better understand the Chinese. A man named John Dewey was living in Peking and he had written many negative articles about China. As an American, perhaps Bufano could go to Dewey and explain the true state of affairs in China.

Benny exclaimed that John Dewey was one of his best friends, that he had studied under him at the University of California and that many times they had talked over chopsticks in San Francisco's Chinatown. Benny knew Dewey to be a fair and honorable man who would listen to Dr. Sun with an open mind; perhaps he might be invited to teach at the University of Canton.

Not only did Dr. Sun invite Dewey to teach at the university, but he invited him to stay at his home, where Bufano enjoyed talking to Dewey.

In a letter to one of the authors, Dewey wrote:

Bufano is markedly individual in his attitudes, but I never thought of him as taking pleasure in being different or disagreeing. He was "Radical" in the sincerity and simplicity of his attitudes but I never thought of him as radical in any sense except that he wanted to do his own thinking, certainly not in the sense that he wanted to be eccentric or to force his views on others. I am sorry I cannot speak more specifically about Benny and Dr. Sun. I feel quite sure, however, that you can trust whatever account he gives you of their relations, how they came together and what they had in common. Of course, I didn't agree with Bufano's ideas. But when I thought he was wrong, I thought it was much more due to limitations in his earlier background than any desire on his part to insist on his own attitudes.

I had forgotten that I stayed at Sun Yat-sen's as much as three weeks; I think Benny was there considerably longer than I was. But my memory for details is defective and for times and dates practically nonexistent. I never had any conversation with Dr. Sun or his wife about Bufano; some anniversary celebrations were going on while I was there of which Sun was the center and he had little leisure, though he himself was so simple he was not at all excited or hurried.

Bufano didn't envy the luxury of Dr. Sun's home, but he did covet the beautiful art objects that filled it. While Benny rambled on through China as a revolutionary, as a potter, as a coolie, as anyone he felt like identifying with, he could not help being impressed with the great works of art all about him. In long letters to Colonel Wood he impressed him with the need of sending more money to buy some of these masterpieces. The money came. What Benny couldn't negotiate on a free basis, he purchased for a relative pittance.

Ingenious Benny found a way of accumulating a large collection for himself. "I had read somewhere," said Bufano, "that the walls of the cities of China had many treasures hidden in them. The story was that the emperor of the Han dynasty, who thought of himself as a supreme being, wanted to destroy all the books of Confucius and the carved gods of the people. When he built the Great Wall of China, the workers, to get even with the emperor, placed the gods and books in the wall for safe keeping. I figured out that the wall of Canton must also have such objects hidden in it. The wall that surrounded Canton was being taken down at this time. By giving the workers a few yen or by sharing my rice with them I got them to let me take the beautiful little figures and carvings which they found in the wall and which, to them, meant nothing." Benny, the artist, knew their worth — without realizing to what degree they would influence his later work.

He bought paintings of the Sung and Ming dynasties; friends gave him beautiful flower studies and portraits and exquisite embroideries. These embroideries were of incredible splendor. One, an enormous birthday hanging, was at one time the property of the Dowager Empress and hung in her palace at Peking; only in the chaos resulting from the revolution could it have made its way into Bufano's possession. The embroidery, done on a background of orange and yellow silk, contained several hundred figures, each one entirely individual both in expression and significance. These enormous hangings, of which Bufano had two, were used only by the greatest nobles or by the royal family and were almost as highly prized, because of the extraordinary beauty of their craftsmanship and design, as were the sculptures and paintings he brought home.

In between his various activities, Bufano often found time to return to the great pottery cities, Shekwan and King-Teh-Chen near Peking, where formerly the imperial pottery for the Manchu emperors was made. But Benny loved Shekwan best of all. Here, in a city of almost 20,000 people, nearly everyone was engaged in pottery making of one form or another. Bufano lived with the potters, ate with them, worked with them; he absorbed everything they knew.

In 1944, twenty-five years later, Benny still worshipped the Shekwan pottery makers. "It is impossible to measure the immeasurable," he said in an address to an art meeting, "to describe the indescribable. With pottery we must speak in the highest language. We can tease people with color in pictures, but the beautiful simplicity of line and color must be in the pottery or it will not meet the test of art. Pottery is the most spiritual of all the arts and links us directly with God.

"Our knowledge of the civilization of the past has come largely through the pottery that has been preserved, for the true potter has always lived close to his people. Indeed, no one should attempt to reproduce the pottery of a people unless he has lived deeply the life of that people."

While staying at the Suns', Bufano took Dr. and Mrs. Dewey to Shekwan, as Benny noted in a letter. He elaborated upon the visit, saying that when they arrived in Shekwan Benny was greeted as "doll maker," the nearest words the potters had for sculptor. Bufano and his friends arrived on a feast day. "It was like they were celebrating the Deweys' visit to their village. I never let on to the Deweys that the celebration wasn't just for them." The next day Benny and the Deweys visited the potteries. "I got a great kick," said Benny, "in seeing Dewey as he watched the foot-driven wheels whirl and the skillful hands turn out small pots and tiny figurines so fast that the eye could hardly follow the movement. It was as though these little works of art materialized out of the clay. Dewey bought 120 of the little figurines." A week after they returned to Canton, Dr. and Mrs. Dewey left for America, but John Dewey had a different attitude toward China, thanks to Bufano and Dr. Sun.

Sun Yat-sen, with his revolution failing, saw the necessity of having a customhouse. He planned to build a new port, to be called Wam Po, about twenty-five miles from Canton. But large sums of money were needed for this project. An auction was decided upon, and poems, paintings and other works by creative artists were donated. Bufano contributed three busts of Dr. Sun; these were the forerunners of the magnificent Sun Yat-sen he was to do for San Francisco years later. The auction was a huge success and enough money was raised to start building the port.

When Bufano was at Hong Kong in 1919 he had met Governor George Hunt of Arizona, who was on his way to Siam as the new American ambassador. Bufano acted as Hunt's guide in Hong Kong, taking him into the byways of the Chinese districts and to Portuguese Macao. Hunt enjoyed Benny's adventuresome spirit and his good humor, and invited Bufano to visit him in Siam soon. "I'd sure like to come," Bufano said, thinking of the great temples of Bangkok. "Maybe you can get the king to invite me!" Through Hunt, the king invited Bufano to come and make a portrait of him. Benny said good-bye to his many Chinese friends, packed his treasures carefully in boxes of straw and took a boat for Siam.

"The king was going to give me $5000 to make his portrait but the guy was so ugly I just couldn't do it with the beauty of those temples and frescoes all around me! I did finish a portrait of Hunt which is in the state capitol at Phoenix."

Bufano looked open-mouthed at the king's graceful barges, carved and gilded; at the prize fights with their vicious kicking, elbowing and punching; the market places with their red-mouthed, betel-chewing old women; the young priests, with saffron-colored robes flowing in the morning sun as they walked with small bowls, begging for their daily bread; the festivals, and the dances.

"I was so excited about the temples and frescoes that I got up early every morning to wander about and fill myself with their beauty. I took Hunt with me to the temple, the Wat Chang, where the priests, in their saffron-colored robes, were singing. Their chanting was very much like the Gregorian chants."

Bufano stayed in Bangkok for four months, adding about fifty small statues to his collection. When the guards weren't around, Bufano didn't mind filching some heads that had fallen from the sculptured bodies and were lying around broken and disintegrating. "Hell," he said, "they were works of art and the king of Siam didn't even know they were being destroyed. At least I appreciated them." While in Siam he took a trip to Cambodia to see Angkor Wat, where he studied the celebrated reliefs representing heroic epics.

Along about this time he got the itch to see Gandhi. Bufano had been reading about the great Indian leader and was deeply impressed with his philosophy. In Canton, while Dr. Sun had been sitting for the portraits Benny was modeling, they had

talked frequently of Tolstoi and of Gandhi as a student and
follower of that great thinker. Dr. Sun had told Bufano that
Gandhi had established an ashram (religious retreat) near War-
dha where the skills of spinning and weaving were practiced
and taught. Benny left Siam and his good friend, Governor Hunt,
fully intending to go to India. But as usual Bufano digressed;
he wanted to gulp down a few added experiences before the
great feast of experience he expected in India. Bufano side-
tripped to the Malay Peninsula, stopping at Singapore for a time,
then went to Java and Bali, where he stayed about six months.

"The Balinese live beautifully in order to die beautifully, and
it is the only place in the world where no money is spent on
entertainment. Everything occurs out in the open for all to enjoy,
and there is no such thing as wealthy groups or poor groups in
Bali. There are absolutely no beggars there. It is the most beautiful island in the world and the Balinese are the most godly
people on earth."

After leaving Bali Benny's first stop was Ceylon. "For five
months I lived with Buddhist monks in the Temple of the Tooth
in Kandy and delved into the translations of Max Müller's 66
volumes of Hindu philosophy."

Arriving in India, Benny wended his way toward the ashram,
in the center of India, but took many side trips to see works of
art on the way. Like a sponge Benny sopped up the sights: the
temples decorated with beautiful murals and stone mosaics, the
murals in the caves and rock temples in Benares, the beauty of
the Taj Mahal in Agra.

"My imagination was aroused when I saw the Pillar of Asoka,
part of a temple that supposedly had been carved from a fallen
meteorite. The 1600-year-old pillar showed no signs of rust. I
got a real kick out of fingering its rough surface. Another thing
that deeply impressed me was the Jain temples, among the most
beautiful in India. Gandhi was born and brought up a Jain. The
Jains are a strict Hindu religious sect which does not permit
the eating of meat, or the use of alcohol or drugs. Any commercial enterprise involving the killing of any animals was not permitted. Their land was a great animal refuge," said Benny. "To

me it's as great a sin to kill humans in war as it is to kill animals for the Jains." Underlying the Jain doctrine is the belief that everything in the universe, including matter, is eternal. Benny mentioned that he was influenced by his study of the Jain philosophy in developing his own concept of immortality, that he will never die.

At last Bufano turned his steps to the ashram of Gandhi, the place of retreat. Here he donned the dhoti and began learning to weave. Gandhi was in the colony at the time, but Bufano did not get to talk to him immediately. Soon it got about that there was a sculptor from America at the ashram and that he had been living in the home of Sun Yat-sen. Gandhi then asked him to visit him in his quarters.

"I found Gandhi in the center of a group of followers, terribly thin and wasted from fasting and living only on a diet of vegetables and fruits. He was dressed in a loincloth or dhoti of homespun and home-woven linen with a shawl draped around his shoulders. Here is the Christ of our age," thought Bufano.

They spoke of Sun Yat-sen, and Gandhi expressed his admiration for that great man, although he did not share all of his ideas. Gandhi explained that he believed in Satyagraha.* "Like Tolstoi, Gandhi thought that all forms of violence were equally wicked. He felt that revolution breeds hatred and violence even though it is based on a good feeling of love for the oppressed. Our social order can only become better when all men have learned to love each other." Bufano wholeheartedly believed this, even though his father had been a Garibaldine. All during his stay at the ashram, while at the loom learning to weave, Bufano thought constantly of the philosophies of Tolstoi, Sun Yat-sen and Gandhi, trying to integrate them into his own philosophy.

He studied the ideas of Gandhi and learned that Gandhi was stimulated not only by the views of Tolstoi but also by the American Thoreau, who was sentenced to serve in a Massachusetts prison because of his "peaceful protest" against the fugitive

---

*Satyagraha: nonviolent disobedience of unjust laws and non-co-operation with the British government.

slave laws. Indeed, it was from Thoreau's essay "Civil Disobedience" that Gandhi borrowed the phrase used widely to describe his program. Thoreau himself had been influenced by the writings of the forest wise men of India who wrote the Upanishads, and somewhere in the early 1800s these great writings were translated. Thoreau had read and pondered them in the Harvard College library. Thus this political technique of boycott and non-violent protest had already crossed and recrossed the ocean to strengthen hearts and to influence minds in India, Asia and North America.

Before leaving the ashram Bufano finished a portrait head of Gandhi, which was later destroyed in a fire that consumed his studio in San Francisco. At the Mahatma's suggestion Bufano took a trip to Madura to see the large, elaborately ornamented temple to Siva, constructed during the Sixteenth Century. From Madura he went to Madras, near the end of 1921. Garbed in the robes of a Brahmanic priest and with the sign of the Brahman, a dot or eye, painted on the center of his forehead, Bufano stepped cautiously over the threshold of the Sacred Temple to Siva in Madras.

Bufano told the story, his eyes sometimes serious, sometimes alight with humor at this youthful escapade: "I know I was a dope to do what I did, but I always wanted to find out things firsthand. I had heard the stories that if any intruder was discovered, it meant certain death. Only a Brahman priest was holy enough to enter. So, I pretended to be deaf and dumb, but I sure wasn't deaf. I could hear the beats of my heart echoing throughout the temple. Trickles of sweat ran down the sides of my face.

"As soon as I got into the temple a swarm of bats began wheeling about my head. The simple beauty of the temple was breath-taking. As I stepped out of the inner temple a group of young worshipers halted me and started talking. I was scared stiff; so I just gestured to them that I could not hear or speak.

"When I look back upon it now, it was sure funny. These people carried garlands of flowers that they usually floated down the river. This time, though, they draped the flowers around my neck. I was sure that this meant I was a dead duck. So I waited for a knife to cut off my head or to be stabbed, but nothing happened. They were really just praying for me because of my affliction. Outside, I breathed a deep sigh of relief, and scooted the hell out of there as fast as I could.

"The experience certainly wasn't worth the risk," he recalled. "It took a week before I fully recovered from that shock." Some days later, back at the ashram, Benny related the story of his temple experience. "The Mahatma was neither sympathetic nor impressed. He said that I was a foolish young man, and recommended that I give vent to my insatiable curiosity in less dangerous ways if I cared to enjoy old age."

Despite the reprimand Bufano continued his eccentric travels in India. "I visited Tagore at his school. He was a shy and silent man with a beautiful face. Sometimes he looked like Christ, much older of course, with a long white beard. Naturally, I was much impressed by his quiet, shy manner. Several times he would recite some of his poetry to me, and at times he would sit in the center and a group of us would sit around him in Hindu fashion and listen. When I was there I was the only outsider. During my stay I read Max Müller's translations of the Upanishads."

Bufano, for a time, fell under the influence of Tagore. However, Bufano was the seeker after truth; he learned that Tagore, who had been knighted by the British in 1915, had returned the title as a protest against Britain's policies in India. Later he reaccepted the title and with it assumed a softening toward the British that turned many of his own people against him.

After seeing Gandhi again for a few days, Benny left for home, but decided to stop off at Japan on the way. As long ago as 1915 he had received an invitation to visit Japan, from a Dr. Yo Hayahara, then high commissioner of the Imperial Japanese government and delegate to the Panama-Pacific Exposition. Benny remembered the invitation and informed Dr. Hayahara that he was in Tokyo.

The doctor invited Benny to visit him on his rice farm in Chuchura, about fifty miles from Tokyo. While with the doctor,

Benny made a portrait bust of his host, who took him to see the temples and places of worship such as the sacred island of Miya Jima. At night the rice boys would gather around and dance the rice dance, asking questions here and there concerning Benny's sculptural works, America, Sun Yat-sen and Gandhi. However, the Imperial government soon learned of Benny's views on peace and began an investigation. They accused him of being an anti-militarist, and within hours he was on his way out of the country.

6 ، The Da Vinci Method

How Bufano got home to San Francisco, other than the fact
that he sailed by ship from the Orient, is not clear. He was non-
committal. In fact, how Bufano got the money to get anyplace
was almost always a mystery. Certainly his friends and occasionally even his enemies offered their financial help — sometimes to get him to a place because he wanted to go, and other
times just to get him out of their hair. But some details of Benny's
life were hard to come by.

On his return to San Francisco, he went immediately to see
Colonel Wood and presented him with several pieces of oriental
art to show his gratitude for financing the trip. He told Wood
of the heroic size of the ancient statues in China, Indo-China
and Siam which started him thinking big; he wanted to com-
bine the ancient art form with the technical development of
modern New York skyscrapers. He had a new idea in sculpture!

Colonel Wood listened with an understanding ear to the
young enthusiast and suggested that the East had met the West
on the ground of art. Said Benny, "If you mean philosophy, they
reach out their hands to us when we are represented by men
like Dewey and Bertrand Russell."

Although Bufano enjoyed talking about his travels and his
developing philosophy, he was anxious to put his thoughts into
action. He went to his old friend, the architect Maybeck, for
whom he had worked during the 1915 Panama-Pacific Exposition, and told him his problems. Maybeck arranged for Benny
to get his own studio in the Palace of Fine Arts as well as a
job as instructor of sculpture at the California School of Fine
Arts. Trouble started immediately! In his first lecture to his

students he pointed to the plaster replicas of Greek and Roman
statuary, which they had been copying under the direction of
their teachers, and said, "To hell with being copy cats! You're
Twentieth-Century Americans. Be modern! Be original! Use the
creative gifts God has given you." When he went to the officials
of the school to ask for some stone, he was told he'd have to
conform to their method of teaching, and they believed in having young students copy the great masters in plaster before
attempting to work directly in any other medium.

"I suppose you want me to bring one of my sculptures here
and let them copy it!" Benny said indignantly.

"Perhaps that wouldn't be a bad idea!" was the answer.

Benny shouted, "What do you think I'm trying to do? Turn
out a bunch of little Bufanos? I'll be damned if I do!"

He told his students that he wanted them to work directly
in hard stone. He told them of an incident that happened when
he was traveling by train in China. "It was raining that day.
As we stopped at one of the stations, I saw a beautiful woman.
She had very little clothing on and her breasts were exposed.
She was cleaning the street. She wore gold anklets, rings and
bracelets, everything that she owned apparently. She was covered with mud because she was sweeping the street.

"Here was a beautiful woman overloaded with a lot of unnecessary jewelry and then the mud. And that's what happens
with most of the sculptors and painters. They forget the basic
elements and begin to load their work with a lot of unnecessary
ornaments. But in hard materials a thing like that is not possible because of the hardness. The great thing about hard material is that it limits your hands and it taxes your brain. Your
hands stop working and your head begins the work. You stick
to the essential forms, whereas you wouldn't in the use of clay
because it's so easy to manipulate."

It was about then that the San Francisco newspapers woke
up to the fact that they had a genius in their midst — not only
a genius, but a young man who wasn't afraid to voice the truths
he had discovered in his lengthy travels and studies. Bufano
became number-one copy for the *San Francisco Bulletin*, the

Daily News, the *San Francisco Examiner,* the *Chronicle* and the throw sheets that existed. The press started calling him "Benny," and he became the darling of the newsmen because of his aphorisms and his controversial opinions on art. This five-foot boy had power. He was unafraid. He had intelligence and said things about art that were provocative. Many of the critics on the papers disagreed with Bufano and spoke in snide, sarcastic words; Bufano hurt inside but did not let on. He enjoyed the notoriety and loved the attention of the newsmen. He wasn't ignored — that was the important thing.

As a precautionary measure against the authorities of the art school, Bufano went to the school at night and smashed the offending plaster casts on the floor, thus making it impossible for the students to copy them. Then he and some students borrowed a truck, stole some stone from the old Mission High School, which was then being demolished, and dumped it back of the School of Fine Arts for the students to use in their work.

When the broken casts were discovered the next morning, an immediate meeting of the directors of the school was called. The verbal battle became so heated that Bufano ended up by yelling, "You're nothing but a bunch of banana peddlers and shouldn't be teaching art to the young!"

For the remainder of the school term, things went from bad to worse until finally in May of 1923 Benny was notified that he had been fired! Bufano told the press: "The entire quarrel arose when Randolph, director of the school and the person with whom I differ materially in school matters, as well as the 'bunch' around him, acted unfairly in the awarding of prizes to students . . . When the judges came together to choose the work for exhibition, they discriminated between the work of students and professionals, giving the latter preference. It seemed to be the name signed to the pieces of art that determined whether the pieces should be shown, rather than the beauty. They try to hold students down. I objected and forced them to allow a great many students' pieces to be selected.

"Randolph didn't like the way I allowed my students in modeling to use their own individuality. He wanted to turn out a

little Bufano or a little Randolph. To me, that was not art. No
one can copy me, nor can I copy anyone else. I taught my students to express themselves in their art. I didn't have them all
follow along like so many sheep, as is the method in vogue in
the art school. To hell with that!

"The little red schoolhouse, the stern schoolmaster who used
the hickory stick, the Babbitt factory that turns out students in
a given pattern, thinking alike, acting alike, these must retire
into history. We must have education for beautiful living and
for the production of beauty in any form, the exaltation of beauty
of line, form, color, thought, the stimulation of creative ability,
to strike a blow at mediocrity and to bring those on Main Street
up to the heights rather than bringing those on the heights down
to the level of Main Street."

Benny left the California School of Fine Arts after calling
the directors a "bunch of mildewed academicians," and they
called him "rebel . . . freak . . . fake." Benny had no job, but
he kept on talking. "People never learn. If they ever want to
keep me quiet, just give me a nice long commission. Work and
talk don't mix." A commission was the lifelong desire of Bufano;
work to do that was paid for.

Bufano's talking began to take on a definite purposefulness;
he wanted to open an art school of his own. "In my school there
will be no one on our faculty who belongs in the banana-peddler
class," he promised. One of his backers, an artist and businessman named Leopold Dreifuss, who would be Bufano's bête noire
for many years, commented, "I am but one of Bufano's many
disciples and am willing to back my judgment financially in
assisting to create in San Francisco a modern school of fine arts
where ability counts."

Bufano opened his own school of art in May; he interested
Princess Donna Santa Borghese, an Italian noblewoman, in help-
ing to organize the school. She was living temporarily in San
Francisco; in Italy she had been an artist, scholar and director
of education. In addition to Princess Borghese and Dreifuss,
Colonel Charles Erskine Scott Wood was also persuaded to help
the school. Characteristic of Bufano, he invited many famous

people to become sponsors, including Tagore, Albert Einstein, Gandhi, Paderewski, Anatole France and Eleonora Duse.

Because Da Vinci — painter, poet, philosopher, sculptor and literateur — had been conversant with all the arts, the school was named the Da Vinci Association. And as Da Vinci correlated all the arts for complete beauty of living, the Da Vinci Association found in him a model for the creation of the new school. The roster of the association included Isadora Duncan, Pamela Bianco, Col. C. E. S. Wood, John Cowper Powys, Witter Bynner, Gertrude Dix, Samuel J. Hume, Arturo Giovanitti, Max Eastman, Sara Bard Field, Ottorino Tonci, Phyllis Ackerman, Gabriele d'Annunzio, Eleonora Duse, Theodore Dreiser, Rabindranath Tagore, Bernard R. Maybeck, Dr. Albert Abrams, Dr. de Danneville, Upton Sinclair, Dr. Sun Yat-sen, Governor George Hunt, Fritz Kreisler, Rachmaninoff and Benedetto Croce. Ironically, one name that was not on the roster was to plague Benny for years to come: Leopold Dreifuss.

On May 28th an article in the *San Francisco Bulletin* commented:

> It's a secret, but art is to be freed! San Francisco is to have an untrammeled Muse that will be let to romp and gambol o'er the easels and pedestals of the new art school. . . .
>
> Freedom will be the slogan of the new school. Bufano, known as the Messiah of the Rebels, will lead them to fame. . . .
>
> The instructors . . . will not criticize the work of their students in the beautiful, oh, so beautiful new studio to be occupied by the school.

Yes, the new studios would be beautiful; they were housed in the Hawaiian Building on the old 1915 exposition grounds. The building, having been put up as a temporary structure, was in disrepair but Bufano engaged the Keystone Commercial Company to do reconstruction and repairs. (He would live to regret this action.)

Examiner columnist Nadia Lavrova wrote in June:

> The Da Vinci Art School was a place in which you found yourself in an immense hall, glass topped, except in places where there is no glass, and sunshine comes pouring in on the bare stone squares.

Columns of the light material used for the Exposition buildings
rise in graceful pseudo-Grecian style. A large group of Neptune
with two of his subordinate Tritons towers over the oval in the
midst of the floor where, according to all precedents, the gold-
fish aquarium must be situated. . . .

The place with its honorable dust of ages (1915 A.D.) looks like
some deserted Venetian palazzo. Quite in keeping with the atmosphere you notice that two of the wings have been transformed
into studios of sculpture and design. The master craftsman and the
soul of the building is Beniamino Benvenuto Bufano.

In discussing his school, Benny said that art "must have in-
tellectual and spiritual freedom in order to attain its highest
development.

"Art is beautiful when it is in harmony with the spirit, it is
not beautiful when it embraces the vulgarities of realism. . . .

"When a man creates a work of art . . . I don't care whether
it is writing or music or painting . . . he is realizing the psycho-
logical drama of his own soul. It isn't the eyes that see or the
ears that hear; it is the mind to which the senses give their report.

"When Leonardo wanted Mona Lisa to smile, he had musicians play for her. You can't divorce art and music. Once I asked
a Chinese artist to draw me a bird. He did it in seven strokes
and, as he made each stroke, he sang a note! I fancy his mind
worked rhythmically, so to speak. Artists have always been lovers
of music. Contour and melody are sisters. Maybe the Chinese
artist got so much pleasure out of what he was singing that it
gave his hand an impetus and a lovely line flowed from the
brush. That is the reason why I am going to have music as
part of my school. I'll have dancing too, all the seven arts. We'll
run a magazine too. One month it will be devoted to some phase
of architecture; another issue will take up an aspect of music,
then the technique of the impressionists. One doesn't need to
swear faith in the Cubists to be interested in their methods or
seek out what message they are trying to give."

The new school had started with high hopes and a few talented students. Redfern Mason, in the *San Francisco Examiner*,
said of Bufano:

. . . the man is mentally alert; his sympathies shoot out in every direction. Like Moliere he takes his fortune wherever he finds it. His is no academic aloofness. Bufano does not impose an aesthetic readymade and complete, on the mind of a disciple, but encourages him to dream his dream, as Carot did, and paint or sculpt that!

Bufano was happy in his new school. It had noble aspirations, and was on the grand scale. Far be it from Bufano ever to be associated with anything small, whether it be statues, aims, purposes or ideals. However, Bufano, the idealist, knew nothing of the practical side of life: bills began pouring in; teachers had to be paid; clay and stone had to be bought; chisels and hammers had to be purchased; trees had to be watered; toilets had to be kept in order and electricity paid for. Benny became involved in a maze of debts until finally the greatest tragedy befell him in October of 1923: his precious oriental collection was attached for the debt incurred for carpentry done by the Keystone Commercial Company. They had sued Benny and received judgment for the sum of $664.55 plus $27.60 for costs. Benny was forced to close his school, rudely awakened from his dream by the ogre of commercialism!

"I have no money and I know nothing of business," he told Colonel Wood. "What am I to do? Maybe I can give my creditors a statue, but to lose one of my treasures would crush me!"

Colonel Wood, a lawyer as well as a man of letters, said, "Maybe I can help you out a bit, Benny."

Somehow the Colonel saved Benny's treasures, but he didn't pay the judgment, because he, too, was close to bankruptcy. Fifteen years of litigation followed. The names of Colonel Wood, the Keystone Company and Leopold Dreifuss became hopelessly entangled with that of Beniamino Bufano. Even Bufano could not unsnarl the vagaries of this part of his life. "I was like a ping-pong ball, banged about by insane players."

7 ′ Preparations for Paris

To compensate for the failure of his school, Benny set to work in his studio as though possessed. He would let nothing interrupt him. He made a group of a mother and two children in stoneware; a terra cotta group in blue glaze called *The Children;* a bust of a Chinese girl in terra cotta; a bust of an old Chinese man in bluish glaze; a small bronze figure with upturned palms; a marble block supporting a bust of Sara Bard Field; a painting in red of children; a bronze bas relief called *Poet in the Desert;* a marble bas relief of three children; a bas relief of Katherine owned by Sara Bard Field; and a bust of Vera Gordon in silver-green stoneware.

Then, as if to repay his efforts, a double triumph was given to Bufano. The Metropolitan Museum of New York purchased *Honeymoon Couple,* and at about the same time the Arden Galleries exhibited his works. Of this showing, the *New York Times* for January 4, 1925, wrote:

> Most of the work in the present exhibition at the Arden Galleries is in his personal medium of glazed pottery. He has modeled two Chinese heads; one is called the "Scholar" and the other the "Philosopher."
>
> Though the models are Chinese, the artist has generalized, until the sense of race is made subordinate to the nature of the learning of each. The color is dull green-blue, the texture smooth and not too shiny, and the outline form is serene as a Chinese bowl, in spite of the necessarily greater variety.
>
> The "Scholar" is dry, and the humor lies in the artist's tolerant point of view toward boundless information, but Bufano and his "Philosopher" can smile together. The "Friends" are tied together by a rhythmic arrangement of line and design. His manner in each case, changes with his subject, without losing style. The subject suggests the manner, and the artist controls both.

The *New York Herald Tribune* stated:

His work comprises a series of portrait busts, small group themes, and a heroic "Crucifixion" . . . his outstanding achievement . . . all done in richly applied colored glazes. He shows in all a visible respect for both the craftsmanship and feeling of ancient Chinese pottery sculpture. But his adaptation of both themes of present-day experience is done with an adroit, personal touch that gives them living qualities.

The large "Crucifixion" which is the most important work of the artist, seems hardly to justify itself. It is quite mechanical and emotionless, though appearing decorative in its wooden frame. Such sculptures find their greatest appeal in the intimacy of design and glaze effects, and in this vein his work takes on a wholly individual and alluring aspect.

Phyllis Ackerman, an art critic writing in the *International Studio* of February, 1925, states in her article, "The East Meets the West!":

A strikingly original contemporary instance of this fusion of two tastes, is the work of Beniamino Bufano.

Bufano does not depend on his hands alone. He works with his convictions and with his aesthetic principles. He has but recently digested his Orient, and it is still formulating his theories. Thus, he is first and persistently a sculptor. And he is remarkably young. With a more complete fusion of his intellect, his technical skill and his emotions, he shows promise of being one of the few enduringly important sculptors that America, if she can claim him, has had.

In San Francisco Bufano, elated by this success, accepted an invitation to attend a party in his honor. Benny, in the style of Ranieri, was drinking a glass of wine with a little lemon peel in it when a young girl sidled up to him. She told him that he was a wonderful artist. Bufano enjoyed the compliment and looked more closely at the girl; he was struck by her bright eyes and the softness of her manner. He thanked her for the compliment. She said she had admired his work for a long time. He asked her name. It was Virginia Howard. A vague memory of Barbara Whitney and the nun Antonia passed through Bufano's mind for the first time in many busy years. During the early months of 1925 Bufano saw Virginia daily.

Beniamino was working on a group of Corona W. Anderson and her four children, for which he was to be paid $3000, and was to deliver a satisfactory plaster-of-Paris copy to Mrs. Anderson. Virginia loved to watch him at his work; she usually sat quietly near him, never interfering with his thoughts. One day she broke the quiet of the studio to tell him that she was leaving San Francisco and moving to Texas. She wouldn't see Bufano any more.

Benny was shocked. What did she mean moving, and for how long?

She was going for good.

Bufano refused to believe her. How could she leave him when they had come to mean so much to each other?

She reminded him that he had told her many times that an artist should not marry. So what was the good of their friendship?

Bufano repeated what he had so often said, that marriage would be a crazy thing for him. It wouldn't be fair to her, either. He would be a bad husband since his work meant more to him than any human being. He would feel tied down and she would be alone most of the time.

She told him over and over again that if they married she would give him all the freedom he wanted. She would not interfere with his work or with his freedom; this she promised him.

He argued that she was hoping for the impossible. She did not realize what kind of man he was. If he decided to go off to China or Timbukto suddenly, he'd go. And she would be alone. He was liable to stay forever wherever he took a notion to stay. That was the kind of man he was.

In that case, she repeated, she would be leaving. If he changed his mind about marriage he could always find her in Texas; she would give him her address. At the end of the week, Virginia was gone and Bufano tackled his work with a vengeance, trying to forget her.

Paul Verdier, owner of the City of Paris, a fashionable department store in San Francisco, had become interested in Bufano. Verdier made preliminary arrangements to have a one-man show of the artist's work in the art gallery in his store. Bufano's understanding of the one-man show was that his art would be exhibited at Verdier's emporium; in return, Verdier would take care of all expenses for an art show in Paris.

Colonel Wood had collected a vast amount of Bufano's art, as collateral on many loans, and agreed to add these works to the Verdier exhibit. But the Colonel was rapidly running out of money, and Bufano would not be able to depend upon him much longer. So, Bufano said, in 1925 he and Wood made a verbal agreement with Verdier on the loan of the art works. (It may sound incredible that Wood, an attorney, would make a verbal agreement, but incredible things often happened around Bufano, particularly when it came to money and finance, or things vaguely referred to as contracts. Contracts would plague Benny for the rest of his life.)

The San Francisco show attracted nationwide art interest. The influence of the ages-old art Bufano had seen in his travels throughout the Orient was evident in the reviews. Gene Hailey, art critic of the *Christian Monitor,* wrote:

> Bufano's paintings, bronzes, porcelains and drawings are presented in a specially arranged gallery with a background of Chinese gold, admirably suited to the rich color of his work. The bronzes and porcelains take on the satisfying hues and tints of the oldest Chinese sculpture.
>
> Bufano's studies have brought him many influences, all of which contribute to his originality of vision. Bufano has not imitated the Orientals so much as he has made them his own, from his sense of true art values. He achieves beauty from his understanding of Oriental symbolism and medieval mysticism, made concrete in sound construction. He is a modernist in his superior understanding of the older arts.

The bronze Crucifixion known as *The Last of the Christians* was named the most important piece in the exhibit. The critics marveled at the calmness of the Christ face, without the usual agony. The entire crucified figure seemed to be as calm as the little children at the feet of the Christ. There was a childlike simplicity in this particular piece, which was its fundamental charm. *The Wasp* of July 11, 1925, attributed maturity to the work and praised the lack of mannerism. There was an atmosphere — purified and chaste — about it. This sculpture gave an expression of Italian tenderness to the austere subject of crucifixion.

These laudatory critiques did not fail to attract the attention of the Keystone Commercial Company, which had received a judgment against Benny for repairs on the Da Vinci school. However, Keystone had not been able to collect, and by July of 1925 the judgment had grown, due to interest and collection costs, to $875. They hounded Benny again for payment.

Bufano, worried that he would lose his life's work and his art collection, again turned to his friend Colonel Wood. The two executed a bill of sale which transferred to Wood 72 pieces of Bufano's own work, plus 104 pieces of art collected by Benny in the Orient. Further, Bufano assigned six pieces of his sculpture to Colonel Wood, who was to pay fifty dollars for them. In the agreement Wood promised to pay off the $875 indebtedness to the Keystone Company. (Records show that Wood never paid Keystone.) The document agreed to allow Bufano to send specified art objects to Paris through Verdier for exhibition, but obligated Bufano to pay all expenses incurred for such an exhibit. This the artist did not understand! Bufano took it for granted that Verdier would pay all expenses for transferring the works of art to Paris and back again to San Francisco. Bufano and Verdier were at the beginning of a long friendship, beset by many squabbles and misunderstandings.

Bufano, believing that this agreement with Colonel Wood took care of all of his indebtedness, blithely went back to work on the Corona Anderson group. Looking at his model of the group, he frowned. He didn't like it. It would look better with only three children; the fourth child was redundant. Benny threw the model on the floor and started a new one. In short order he had recomposed the group: Mrs. Anderson no longer was the mother of four children. Benny had purged the fourth!

As he was looking at it with a grin of creative satisfaction, Mr. Anderson entered the studio. He stalked up to the model, looked at it, then shouted, "What the hell's going on here! Where's my baby?"

"Oh him," said Bufano. "I clipped him off."

"You what!?" Mr. Anderson looked horrified.

"I clipped him off," Benny said casually.

"Listen, Bufano. I've got *four* children and you signed a contract to do my wife with all of our children. And that's what I want. You're not clipping off anything!"

"The hell I'm not," said Benny. "I'm the artist and I'll do what I think is right."

"I'll never pay you a red cent for this," said Mr. Anderson grimly. "Not until you put my baby back."

Bufano did a rare thing; he compromised. "Okay, Mr. Anderson. I'll put the kid back. Come back in a few days and I'll show you a new model."

A week later Mr. and Mrs. Anderson stared unbelievingly at the new model. "But you left out my baby again," said Mrs. Anderson furiously.

"Oh no I didn't," Bufano said happily. He turned the model around and there on the back he pointed to the child carved on a tiny medallion hanging from a small chain on the mother's neck.

"On her back! Are you crazy?" asked Mr. Anderson.

Benny shrugged his shoulders. "It's all how you look at it. The Chinese peasant woman carries her baby on her back. You get new ideas when you go to the Orient. You'd better go to China, Mr. Anderson."

Mr. Anderson stormed out of the room — another contract shattered — leaving Bufano bewildered at the injustice of human behavior. The Andersons finally settled with Bufano by paying for the model. They did not, however, have it cast in bronze or terra cotta, or carved in marble, as was the original plan.

"I can't understand why people are so unreasonable," Bufano said, after collecting the money.

While all such misunderstandings did not make the newspapers, Benny's popularity with the press continued and increased as time passed. He was usually good for a story and more than willing to oblige reporter friends with lively copy. They wanted to know more about him: Where and when was he born? And his parents — who were his mother and father? How many children were there in his family? How had he got to America?

Bufano told the story of his birth as his mother had told it to him. "I was born in San Fele, a town named after San Felicia, the patron saint of peace.

"San Fele's the shape of a cone . . . all steps," said Bufano, holding his hands high above his head, work-hardened fingers touching, as he described his birthplace. His sentences came clipped, with the faintest nuance of an Italian accent. "Hardly any level section, except the piazza and where the houses sit. The whole town is on a mountain." He described everything as though it were a piece of sculpture.

"All day long donkeys and horse-drawn carts used to wander up the street and around the hills. That's how the people got around — unless they walked. It's about the same now, except there's a bus that doesn't run. I had a terrible time getting into the town when I went back there — couldn't get transportation. It's like that town in the book *Christ Stopped at Eboli*. It's one of the little towns that are completely forgotten. They don't have a saloon or movie on every block, but they do have little wineshops and restaurants. It's a wonderful little town and everybody knows each other. It's a Catholic town, but the Communists and Catholics live right next to each other and work together, like in that movie about Don Camillo.

"Our house was on a street at the entrance to the town, set in a chestnut grove. It had an attic and a wine cellar. The people gathered the chestnuts and roasted them, and my mother put them in the attic. When we'd have guests in the winter time, we'd serve the chestnuts with wine, like the Japanese and Chinese serve tea. Our house was a big house — fourteen rooms. We had lots of kids, fifteen of 'em. I was the fourteenth, I think!"

Benny's eyes twinkled and he grinned, explaining that the priest, at the time of baptism, refused to baptize him into the Catholic faith because of his unchristian name. Papa and Mama Bufano were not ones to be coerced into changing the name, so the baptism did not take place. This never bothered Benny particularly; he admits his religion is somewhat unorthodox, if not altogether confusing. "I must be an eclectic. I try to find the good in all religions . . . Christian, Buddhist, Mohammedan, Jewish . . . all of them."

Beniamino never knew for sure the year of his birth. Lucrecia insisted it was 1898; Canio argued it was 1900. Benny, in a quandary about his birth date, finally settled the matter by siding with his mother whom he loved passionately. "She ought to know," he would say. "She was there. Anyhow, Papa loved to argue, especially with Mama. He'd argue that I never was born at all, if he thought he could get a rise out of Mama, and believe me, he always did!"

Lucrecia had proudly told her son that his birth cry was a volcanic challenge, as though he said, "Here I am world! I am no ordinary child of man. I am one who will be heard!"

Canio was at home when Benny was born and heard the explosive cry of his newborn son. He entered the room where Lucrecia lay with her child beside her. He looked at the wizened little face. "Basta!" he exploded. "He's a runt! A little runt!"

Lucrecia protested. "But he's strong, Canio. He has strong lungs."

Canio shrugged his shoulders.

Lucrecia, seeing the skepticism in her husband's eyes, decided to administer the coup de grace. "St. Francis was short, Canio! And Garibaldi wasn't tall either!"

As always, this made Canio angry. "Garibaldi! He was the great liberator! The great hero of Italy! It doesn't matter that he was short or tall!" Canio had belonged to the Garibaldini faction, which wanted to dethrone King Humberto and establish a republican form of government in Italy.

Lucrecia, too tired to argue, knew in her heart that this little boy would become a great fighter like Garibaldi. She named him Beniamino — "son of my right hand."

Through the years, the newspapers fed these facts out to the public as they became known. Hundreds of articles appeared, sometimes exaggerated or colored to suit the imaginations of the writers. Familiarity led to the name he has been called in San Francisco ever since — Benny. The police called him Benny; the citizens called him Benny; everyone called him

Benny. To some he became a comic-strip character. Benny, the great artist and nonconformist, became a byword. Readers watched their newspapers for new escapades or humorous episodes in the life of Benny. Bufano liked this and hated it at the same time. He loved the publicity, but in his room at night humiliation came to him. Then, the hope was born of doing something so great for San Francisco that it would overcome even the most snide articles. He would make a colossal statue of St. Francis for one of the hills in the city.

Bufano asked his artist friends to write to the San Francisco Art Commission on his behalf for a commitment to create such a statue. He was sure that his beloved city would never refuse a sculpture of the good St. Francis, patron saint of San Francisco. Benny forgot that politicians and city bosses might consider purse strings when it came to art. His friends wrote to the Art Commission but Bufano was far away when the answer was given.

In 1925 the papers and periodicals were busy with a new idea called "companionate marriage." This was a trial marriage which could be dissolved at the end of a year at the desire of the parties to the marriage. This concept was the result of the evils of the double standard for women and the many divorces that occurred. Bufano, like other youths, was thoroughly absorbed in this new philosophy.

The year 1925 had been a good one for Bufano. Although he loved the fine critiques and the adulation of the art lovers, he was contemptuous of museums and art galleries. He expressed himself in strong terms to the newspapers and to his friends: "Museums are the graveyards of the artist. They are the death warrants which accompany the artist to his grave. The museum director is the artists' gravedigger, and where he leaves off the merchants take over. The museums and art galleries live solely off the artist. These institutions are the black widow spiders who eat their benefactors after the show is over." Perhaps it was the gnawing and the loneliness for Virginia and his desire to see her that made him so bitter about the galleries, which at that time were being very kind to Bufano.

He consulted with Ansel Adams, a young photographer with whom he had made friends. Adams was as poor as Bufano and could think of no way of Benny's getting to Texas where Virginia had fled. Bufano thought of going to Colonel Wood, but Benny had spoken so often to him about the stupidity of artists marrying, that he felt embarrassed about seeing The Old Gentleman. Benny finally hit on an excuse for going to Texas that had nothing to do with Virginia. He went to his friend in Los Gatos and told Wood that he wanted to go to Texas to study the cotton-field Negroes for one of his sculptures. He asked for the loan of "a few bucks."

Colonel Wood was not deceived by Beniamino's subterfuge and wanted to know if the Negroes up in San Francisco were different from those down in Texas.

Benny pretended not to understand what Wood was implying and answered that the Negroes of Texas were different in their posture and that he wanted to capture their special posture as they leaned over to pick the bolls and sang as they went along.

Wood knew there was no stopping Bufano once he wanted to do something, so arranged with his bank to take care of the expenses.

Within hours of arriving in Texas Bufano was with Virginia. If she insisted on being married, he wanted only a trial companionate marriage for three months; by then they would know if they really loved each other. Virginia was sure that she loved him and was willing to go into the marriage on a trial basis. Beniamino and Virginia were married and returned to San Francisco. Within three months, Bufano knew that he could not tolerate the restrictions of marriage.

Later, in commenting on the separation, Virginia said, "To defy convention is to place one's self at the mercy of a world that does not understand. Bufano did not desert me. He was absorbed in his art . . . in works of genius. He was an exquisite husband."

In answer to this, Bufano said, "She's crazy! I was a lousy husband."

Early in 1926, anxious to get away from his domestic trouble, he went to Los Gatos to see The Old Gentleman again. He told Wood that Paul Verdier was planning to send the exhibit of his works all over the United States before they finally went to Paris. Benny wanted to be at the opening in Paris, in 1928, but thought he would take a few side trips on the way. He had over a year and could get a lot of studying done.

Wood wanted to know if he intended to stop in Texas again. Beniamino grinned and said not this time. He thought he would go to Africa.

Wood, always the attorney, asked what he was going to do about his art objects and sculptures. Bufano had a ready answer. He was wondering if they couldn't bury all his stuff someplace for safe keeping on the Colonel's estate. Colonel Wood laughed so loud and so long that Bufano was afraid The Old Gentleman might die of a heart attack. Wood called him "Beniamino the Pirate" who wanted to bury his treasure. When would they start?

Benny was never at a loss: right that minute — he had a moving van with all of his stuff out in front of the house. Bufano led the way to a far corner of the estate, the serious Colonel following. Benny pointed to a spot and said he thought this place would do. But Wood insisted that they write up an agreement and, since this was a blood-and-thunder story, they would sign it in blood. Beniamino told the Colonel he looked like Jove and would probably start hurling thunderbolts. The agreement was signed and sealed, and for days Benny and Colonel Wood dug holes and buried Bufano's treasures.

In later life Bufano used the hand to symbolize peace. This one, of copper and mosaic, with stained glass over the tips of the fingers, stands in Quail Court, Walnut Creek, California.

Bufano paid tribute to the great thinkers and humanitarians of our age by casting their likenesses in heroic statues and mosaic portraits. This mosaic of Einstein is at the International Gallery, San Francisco.

Shadows of the Future, carved from black granite in 1919, is now at the Stanford University.

St. Francis on Horseback, in black granite, is a rare one-piece equestrian statue presently on the mall at the Hillsdale Shopping Center, San Mateo, California.

This portrait in glazed stoneware, of Mrs. Walter Haas and her children, is now at the Cory Galleries, San Francisco.

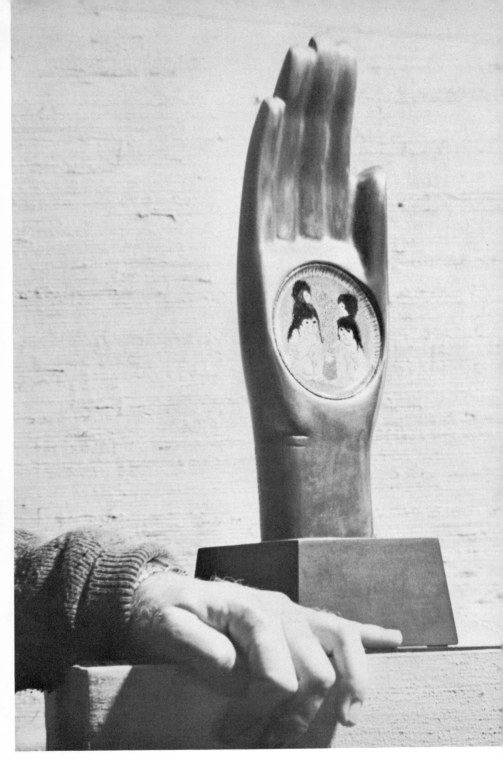

Many copies of this small hand of peace were cast. Because of its size, the insert was made of ceramic, not mosaic.

Bufano happily participated in the unveiling of his *Madonna* at an exhibit of "Church Art Today," at Grace Cathedral, San Francisco, in 1960.

Bufano first used "mosaics in the round" in the figures of Joseph and Mary. The statues are presently at the Alcoa Building in San Francisco, along with several animal sculptures. The oval and sphere in the foreground is an untitled work of his in bronze and mosaic.

This female torso in granite, one of the few that Bufano ever produced, is currently on display at the Cory Galleries.

St. Francis de la Varenne, which Bufano carved in a Paris suburb in the late 1920s, has a long history of neglect and controversy. The statue now stands in front of the I.L.W.U. Memorial Hall, near Fisherman's Wharf in San Francisco.

Bufano's *Sun Yat-sen,* made of red granite and stainless steel, commemorates the Chinese revolutionary leader, whom Bufano met in China in the 1920s. The statue, completed under the W.P.A. in 1937, stands in St. Mary's Plaza, San Francisco.

This casting for the head of a St. Francis, similar to the one at The Cannery in San Francisco, was destroyed by vandals in the artist's studio.

When Bufano's studio at Big Sur was vandalized, among the works destroyed was a model for the statue of St. Francis that he hoped to see on Twin Peaks. The arms that were to be raised in benediction over San Francisco are shown here, broken at the elbows.

At another vandalized studio, Bufano studies his broken, toppled and defaced models.

At The Cannery in San Francisco stands this imposing St. Francis of metal and mosaic. The hands are spread as a gesture of peace rather than raised in benediction.

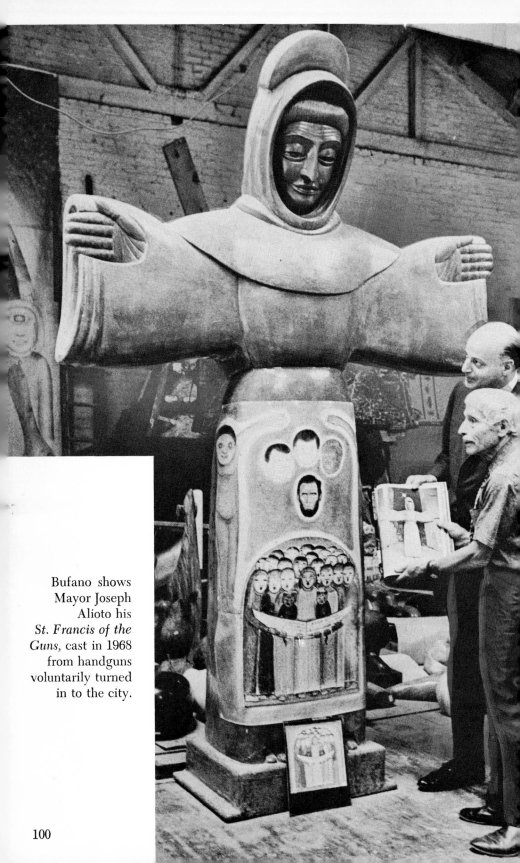

Bufano shows
Mayor Joseph
Alioto his
*St. Francis of the
Guns,* cast in 1968
from handguns
voluntarily turned
in to the city.

8 · Paris and St. Francis

It was 1926 before Bufano started on his journey, ostensibly to get to Paris in time for his exhibit but also to find a piece of granite for his proposed St. Francis. Ever since he had won the $500 prize in the contest in New York, Bufano felt sure that he would never be denied, and that his St. Francis would be accepted and stand high on one of the hills of San Francisco. Now that the critiques on his works had been so laudatory, even the slightest doubt had left him.

Impulsive Benny made his usual side trips first to see the Hopi Indians with his old friend Governor Hunt, then by ship through the Panama Canal to the Gold Coast, then to Burma, Peking, Lhasa and Tibet. He became so absorbed in the new sights and sounds that he almost forgot the original purpose of his journey, but he still managed to find time to go to Assisi to study the life of the saint he planned to model.

Always Bufano carried in his bag fifty or more copies of the Little Blue Books, his chief source of reading material and study on his travels. On the train to Pisa the Fascist police, "always on the alert, examined my dinky luggage and found my saddle bag almost filled with these small books. I tried to explain, in Italian, what they were, but since the booklets were written in English, they wouldn't believe me. They clapped me in jail, suspecting me of carrying leaflets opposed to the Mussolini regime," said Bufano. "Hell, that damned fascist! I hated him but I didn't let on.

"I finagled permission from the police department to call Princess Borghese in Bologna. I reversed the charges and told her what had happened. The next day she came to the jail and got me released. But they told her I couldn't leave Italy because my passport had run out. I had been so busy traveling around that I never even gave a thought to such stupid crap. They took my passport away."

The Princess took him to Bologna where he stayed with her in her palace. She contacted the mayor of Bologna, with whom Benny became good friends, and in short order the passport was retrieved, renewed and returned to its owner.

Benny went to Assisi, where he arranged to live in a Franciscan monastery to learn the way of life of the followers of St. Francis and to absorb the deeply religious and medieval atmosphere still pervading the town. He spent long hours in the two Gothic cathedrals built over the tomb of the saint and studied the beautiful frescoes, done by Giotto and others, which decorated the churches. In the convent's library he found many exciting books on St. Francis. His favorite was entitled *Fioretti di San Francisco (Little Flowers of St. Francis)*, in which Benny read the many beautiful stories, built up around the saint, exemplifying his love of nature and of man, a love so great that St. Francis once preached to the birds. Bufano also memorized the "Cantico del Sole" ("Hymn of the Sun"), which the saint may have written, and in which his spirit breathes. Beniamino thought of his mother very often, remembering her love of the good St. Francis. When Benny left Assisi, he was imbued with the spirit of the saint and inspired with a plan to do a twenty-foot statue of him to be erected in San Francisco.

In Paris, he looked up Paul Verdier who had an office there. Verdier let him have a room in the basement of the building, but Bufano needed a studio as well.

Verdier told him that Paul Manship, the sculptor, was in town. Perhaps Benny knew Manship?

Of course Bufano knew Manship. Hadn't he done Manship's enlargements for the 1915 exposition? Bufano contacted Manship, who told him that he used his studio only during July and August and that Benny could use it the other months. Until the time of the opening of his exhibit, he worked in Manship's studio on models for his St. Francis.

Letters were forwarded to him from all parts of Africa, China and from Assisi, but Bufano was too busy to bother either reading or answering his mail. St. Francis was his obsession, day and night. He was excited and didn't want to be distracted. Mail could wait but St. Francis couldn't. Bufano pictured him in cruciform design standing on Twin Peaks, blessing the City.

The Paris exhibit of Bufano's work opened in 1927 with a special preview. On November 1, the Paris correspondent of the *New York Times* sent a special cable to New York:

> Paris, October 13. Mr. Johannes, President of the jury of the Autumn Salon which opens in the Grand Palais next Saturday, predicted today that the sensation of the approaching exhibition would probably be the work of the young American sculptor of Italian origin, Beniamino Bufano. "His work is widely discussed at the present time and he is incontestably a very beautiful artist," said Mr. Johannes. Generally speaking, the exhibition will register another unmistakable step away from the fantastic "isms" of recent years and back to the truly beautiful and objective in art.

Mr. Johannes' speculation as to the critical results of the Bufano exhibit was prophetic. Roger Fry, the noted English art critic wrote:

> Bufano has achieved a new freedom in his simplification of form and movement. In his stony rich forms one feels the firmness of the stone. Note that in his simplification he has discovered a curious method of rounding off the transition, from one plane to another, and at the same time holding firmly to the main structural unity. There is none of the decorative tightness of folds, muscles, or tricky detail. There are no accents to mark the division of planes. The absence of all detail and accents is replaced and graced by a continuous flow of pure form and line, producing an admirably balanced system of flowing masses. A slow tempo of movement and change making this great sculptor the outstanding innovator of his time amongst sculptors. . . .
>
> Notice the extraordinary calmness and the penetrating silence that the absence of detail betrays; a quality that only great sculpture can claim. Note the quietude and the extraordinary simplicity of the black granite group of the two kneeling figures . . . how the arm in the back is rendered close to the main form of the body so as to keep intact the sculptural beauty. This innovation in sculpture has never appeared before anywhere in the history of sculpture and will be most illuminating to sculptors. . . . In his portrait . . . Heads of Children . . . he is at his best. Portraitures

of glazed stone terra cottas . . . if they can be called portraits . . .
because of the freedom that he takes with them; this very human
side of him betrays his gentleness and tenderness . . . a simplicity
that is only found in children.

Bufano, in a talk with Roger Fry, said, "I love to do children
because they never worry about their likeness and a child never
asks me silly questions. I love to do them because they help me
to be a sculptor and not just a portrait maker."

Aristide Maillol, the great French neoclassic sculptor who
had been inspired by early Greek sculpture, said of Bufano, "A
great sculptor . . . and so young. I am glad for America she has
given us one great sculptor!"

Overnight, Bufano became an international figure in the world
of art! The cultured aristocracy of Paris awoke to the fact that
a great artist was in their midst. Benny was honored at fetes
given by social leaders such as the Comtesse de Castelbajac.

Although the French exhibit was a great artistic triumph it
was not a financial success. From Paris, Benny was carrying on
a heated exchange of letters with Paul Verdier, who had returned
to San Francisco. On the first of January, 1928, he wrote Verdier:

> I reluctantly consented to allow my things to be exhibited in your
> store under the one and only condition that they were to be
> brought here to Paris to be exhibited at your expense, and there-
> after to be returned to San Francisco in absolute safety, likewise
> at your expense . . . all to which you agreed. Because I took you
> to be a man of your word and trusted you with the faith of a
> child, I did not insist upon a legal document setting forth the
> terms of our agreement. But, unfortunately for you, there are suf-
> ficient witnesses to our verbal contract, to hold you to it by law.

The heat of Bufano's anger still reached boiling point when he
thought of the 1915 Panama-Pacific Exposition and the unfair
treatment he had received. Now, he hit back at his friend Verdier.
His knowledge of law was still childish and that of the layman.
What seemed reasonable to him must be the law! All the ramifi-
cations of legal terms meant nothing to him. Bufano saw only
his side of the picture.

Verdier was of a contrary opinion, that he had not obligated
himself to return the pieces to San Francisco. He therefore sug-

gested that Bufano enlist the aid of several people of financial means in San Francisco.

In answer to this Benny wrote:

> The very thought of soliciting money from Herbert Fleishhacker [banker and patron of the arts], and Colonel Wood for the purpose of defraying the expense of shipping my things back to San Francisco is as prepostrous as it is ridiculous! If you write to them for money, do so on your own accord. . . . Do not mention my name. I do not do things in that lowly fashion! But I advise you not to write to Mr. Wood. He would only laugh at you and then settle his account with you in his own direct fashion!

> I hold you and only you responsible for the return, in absolute safety, of Mr. Wood's things and my things, to San Francisco, and I advise you for your own good, to do this at once.

Bufano took a final stab at Verdier by saying:

> You intimated to me your belief that Mr. Wood had purchased his things from me while they were on exhibition at your store in San Francisco; that he and I had defrauded you out of the commission of the purchase. This was an unkind mistake on your part. Your insinuation was not only directed to myself, but to my friend, Mr. Wood; at that time I wrote to Mr. Wood telling him of your belief. In answer to my letter, he suggested writing you, but I discouraged him, saying it was not worth the trouble.

How Bufano got his treasures back to San Francisco he kept a mystery. Most likely some wealthy friend came to his rescue, as usual: accepting money from the rich never bothered Bufano. He felt that the artist belongs to the world and the world should pay his expenses happily. Unfortunately, not all the rich had the same point of view. This led to tragedies in the life of Bufano.

With the sculptures safely on their way to San Francisco, Bufano joined a group of artists in organizing a new avant-garde magazine, *Le Cercle et Carré*. Among the artists who belonged to the group were Fernand Leger, Piet Mondrian, Paul Klee and Carlo Carra, all familiar to present-day art lovers; some of them were famous in 1928, others were still unrecognized, poor and often hungry. Bufano designed the cover for the magazine: a black background with a red circle on it and within the circle a black square. (He used the same design for the cover of an art book of his works published in Florence in 1956.) The circle means the universe and the square means the earth — space and earth.

Most of the artists wrote articles about either their work or their philosophy. They also wrote about their gripes and the hardship of their lives, and met to talk at the famous little Cafe du Dome, which was usually full of exciting people: artists and art lovers and those who wanted to mix with the art world. They also met at L'Escargot and La Rotund. Theirs were the voices crying in the wilderness.

In one of his articles Benny wrote:

> The next fifty years will be the greatest the world has ever known. I am grateful to science. The new materials of science are a feast and a challenge to the imagination of the artist. I am glad that I am living in the greatest and most enlightened age that ever was, in spite of our shortcomings, because we know our greatness and knowing this, we shall overcome our faults.

The group of artists and literary people living in Paris met not only for cultural reasons, but primarily to try to do something constructive for the creative person. "All the great ones used to drop in," said Bufano. "Gertrude Stein and Ernest Hemingway were among them. We tried to frame laws so that the creative artist wouldn't be cheated. Take Modigliani, for instance. He died when very young, about thirty-six, and the most he ever got for his paintings was seventy-five francs. There was one art merchant in particular who, guessing that Modigliani would be great one day, used to feed him Pernod and sardines in return for his paintings. Then after Modi died this art collector made millions on him. That's the story I got from Madame Rosalie." * Benny was always bitter about the treatment of creative artists throughout the world. To him, no one properly understood the creative person except another creative person. "Inwardly, a creative artist is a complicated maze," he believed, "like a sponge of radioactive particles absorbing every element in the constant changing and moving force of this thing we call life."

---

*Mme. Rosalie owned a small restaurant in Paris.

Nights, Bufano loved to take part in the talks and discussions with the artists connected with *Cercle et Carré*. Days, he worked on his sculpture; his visit to Assisi was bearing fruit.

It was mid-November of 1927, and the bitter cold of the Continental winter was no respecter of artists. It rained, it snowed, and the winds howled over the fields outside of Paris in the town of La Varenne, St. Hilaire, a suburb of Paris. Perched high on a scaffolding in the middle of the field, chipping away at three enormous blocks of black granite and singing the "Cantico del Sole" at the top of his lungs, was Beniamino Bufano. No studio, however large, and no floor, however strong, could hold a statue eighteen feet high and weighing twelve tons. This was Bufano's *St. Francis de la Varenne*. He had found the great piece of black granite, chosen for its hardness, just what he needed for the statue. His enthusiasm and excitement was shared by his good friends, the Collinses, who bought it for him. Benny didn't wait for commissions. If he wanted to do a sculpture he took it for granted that its beauty would be so overpowering that no one could resist buying it.

When asked by the authors if he made many drawings before he started a sculpture, Bufano replied: "I make a lot of drawings of the things I'm going to do but I never make a drawing of the thing itself. I try to make them backwards, sideways, so that I will know what I'm going to do when I go to work on the statue. They're just work drawings.

"I made about two thousand drawings while I was in Paris during the late twenties. I scheduled myself to make at least three drawings a day, and if I didn't do three, I would tax myself by not eating for two days. I used to sip coffee and eat a croissant or a brioche and make these drawings. They were line drawings. I don't like to use the word 'sketch' because I don't make any sketches. They're complete line drawings. I don't have many drawings left, as most of them were destroyed in one of my fires. I was burned out by the politicians, and nobody can tell me otherwise, because I attacked them and exposed them for what they really were.

"If I didn't make those drawings in the cafe, I would go back home, get in bed, cover myself up because it was cold — and there's nothing colder than Paris in the wintertime — and then I'd make the drawings. In addition to my St. Francis, I also did some other large sculptures. Two of these large sculptures are now in Mills College. I also made a sort of semi-abstract portrait of Princess Borghese's child in black diorite, and several others as well."

In all, he worked for fourteen months on the *St. Francis de la Varenne*, dreaming of the time when his beautiful statue would stand on one of the hills of San Francisco. Hunger and bleak cold during the winter were the fate of the young artist. He had traveled light, as usual, and had with him only one suit, a leather jacket, two pairs of socks and an old pair of shoes. Benny shivered and his hands went numb. He blew on his hands to warm them. He wore the leather jacket over his suit coat but the icy blasts still penetrated. He always brought his lunch — a loaf of bread, a hunk of cheese and a small bottle of wine. This meager meal was provided by Madame Rosalie. When he finished work for the day there was the trip back to Paris in the cold bus. How welcome was the cup of hot coffee Madame Rosalie gave him when he reached her cafe, blue with the cold.

Through all of these tribulations, the bright dream of the time when his St. Francis would overlook the Bay brightened his spirits and he sang on and on. But at times with the cold came a lowering of his spirit and a small doubt. He was tempted to go to Manship's studio where his mail was accumulating and satisfy himself that all was well in San Francisco. He didn't go. Once, when doubt assailed him, Benny pleaded with Madame Rosalie to go with him to La Varenne. She went and stood shivering at its feet looking up at the great statue, admiring its strength and beauty.

She told him no people in their right minds would reject it. However, she added, Americans were an outlandish people and you couldn't know what they would do. He'd better look at his mail.

Bufano was stubborn. When he was finished he'd look at his mail and prove to her that Americans were not outlandish and would accept his *St. Francis de la Varenne*.

Roger Fry made a trip to La Varenne to see the statue. His verdict was: "Bufano's huge black granite statue of Saint Francis of Assisi is the most significant piece of sculpture done within five hundred years. A truly great contribution to a great saint."

Finally, the statue was finished. Bufano opened the stack of letters that had accumulated in Manship's studio. San Francisco had failed him! His sketches had been rejected! Disillusioned and heart-broken, he spoke to the members of *Le Cercle et Carré*. They immediately passed judgment on the people of the United States: they were a benighted lot lacking in artistic understanding. Bufano would do better to stay in Paris where his works had had great recognition. Benny suggested that perhaps Paris would accept the statue. They looked a little embarrassed and ceased their criticism of Americans.

"I was desperate," Bufano recalled. "I had to consult my only real friend, Madame Rosalie. To her, an artist was an artist, whatever his place of birth. She was our friend. To earn a few pennies and my meals, I had been cooking in the tiny restaurant on the Rue Delambre, run by Madame Rosalie and named after her. Rumor had it that she had been in love with Renoir and had even given birth to a son by that famous artist. Madame Rosalie, now eighty years old, never denied the story, but permitted a sly smile to cross her lips whenever she reminisced about Renoir. Here, in this tiny restaurant, she still babied the artists, gave them food, praised their work and scolded them."

Madame Rosalie was the confidante of all the artists, and through the years she listened to the moanings and complaints of Modigliani, Utrillo, Picasso, Leger, Klee and many others. Now she was sympathizing with Benny about his St. Francis being left unprotected in the bare, cold fields outside of Paris. As Benny told it, Madame Rosalie literally grabbed him by the hand and pulled him along after her, much as she would have dragged her own child. Occasionally she swore at Benny and with each oath she jerked him all the more. Finally she brought him to a

large brick building in one of the industrial sections of Paris
and presented him to the owner.

The man shrugged his shoulders. Having known Rosalie and
her destitute artists for many years, he knew what he was in for.
A favor was wanted. He put his hand in his pocket for a few
francs.

Madame Rosalie said no, it was not that. Something much
simpler than that. All she wanted was to use some of his storage
space.

Bufano remembered the man's look of relief. Storage space
he had. The little corner over there could be used, or maybe
even the space behind the desk?

Oh, no, much more than that, said Benny. It was for a statue.

Maybe it could be put on one of the tall shelves in the back?

Madame Rosalie told him the statue was eighteen feet high.

Eighteen feet? Mon dieu!

And twelve tons at least, added Bufano.

This the owner would not do. It would wreck his building.
Besides, it would have to be hauled. No man could carry it. That
would cost money, lots of money. No, no, no, he couldn't help
out!

Madame Rosalie sat down and began to sob. Monsieur, for
the first time, had disappointed her. He must be getting old and
heartless. She broke into hysterical crying as Monsieur tried to
ignore her, and between her sobs she winked at Benny.

Two days later an enormous truck with a crane lumbered out
to the fields, lifted St. Francis onto the truckbed and lumbered
back to the warehouse where the statue would lie, awaiting its
fate, for more than a quarter of a century.

"Madame Rosalie was a great woman," said Bufano. "She had
this restaurant for many years. At night, the artists used to sleep
on her restaurant benches, and they'd all make paintings of
things they saw around there and give them to her. She was a
wonderful lady but as tight as the devil with her money. I think
the restaurant still runs today, even with her name, but I heard
that mainly American tourists go there.

"She was a wonderful lady, but she had a tough break. After Modigliani died, the prices for his art went sky-high. Even a few scratches of his were worth hundreds of dollars. When she learned how valuable her collection of his works was, she thought she was a rich woman. She went down to the cellar, opened the door and lo and behold the rats had eaten up all the drawings. The poor old lady cried. The only thing left was a mural that Utrillo had made on her wall. She finally got five thousand francs for that. She hated the art dealers because they and not the artists made the money. She used to cry a lot about the way Modi died in 1920."

Bufano knew women superficially. "I don't think I was ever attached to any of them. I was too busy with my work. I always liked older women anyway, like Madame Rosalie. There was another one, a Madame Vasiliev, a tiny Russian woman who had a restaurant in Paris where she had entertained Lenin and Trotsky when they were in exile. Madame Vasiliev, a woman of talent, was one of the interesting women of that day. She made delightful puppets and primitive paintings and was known to all the artists of Paris. I also used to go to a woman named Magda who was a wonderful cook. At her house I met Princess Desirée who taught me how to make a very wonderful dessert. I made it many times for Harry Hopkins, who used to say, 'Each time you eat it you have to lick your fingers.'

"It's very simple to make. Get bananas that are not too ripe, cut them in half and fry them in butter with brown sugar and a little honey. The bananas should not be soft, remember that. Then put them in a chafing dish and pour brandy over them and burn the brandy out — a little expensive because of the brandy, but a wonderful dessert. President Roosevelt didn't like it too much, but Hopkins was crazy about it. So was Magda in Paris. She was a very wonderful gal. She got married to a singer in New York. He made his living while in Europe as a bullfighter. A wonderful guy. He was a singer, studying opera. Can't imagine a guy studying opera and getting all bruised up being a bullfighter. We had more fun over that."

Benny always enjoyed himself. He extracted fun out of everything he did, and even in the most calamitous situations his sense
of humor often prevented a calamity from becoming a tragedy.
But the rejection of St. Francis was sheer tragedy: his high hopes
had crumbled when he saw the statue lying near a wooden wall
in the warehouse. The tragedy of rejection right after the elation
of praise from the greatest critics brought frustrated anger and
dreadful disappointment. As the years passed, Bufano learned
to accept rejection and defeat with a shrug of the shoulder when
in public. Alone in his room, there would come a deep groan of
hurt and dismay, followed by tears that washed away the sorrow.

Bufano begged, borrowed and stole some gunny sacks with
which he wrapped his beloved statue. He ran his winter-rough-
ened hand over the sculpture in farewell and left, wondering if
he would ever see it again.

He left Paris and went to visit the Collinses in Cagnes Sur
Mer, where he set to work on porphyry and made a red porphyry
bull and two camels which his British friends said would be put
in the British Museum.

"While we were in Cagnes Sur Mer," said Bufano, "we had
week-end workshops. George Antheil was there, John and Pat
Cunningham, Schoenberg used to come down; James Joyce and
a number of other people. Every Saturday night we'd read from
Shakespeare for a while and then from Joyce. Each of us would
improvise; for instance, George Antheil would play the piano,
then Schoenberg would improvise a composition, and a man by
the name of Link Gillespie would read some of his telescopic
words, and then James Joyce would really show us how to read
his rather esoteric writing."

But this diversion was only temporary; Bufano, in the quiet
of the night, thought of his St. Francis lying prone and gathering dust in the warehouse in Paris. His high hope had ended in
terrible disappointment. Fortunately he did not know that
twenty-five years later his statue, like its prototype the good
Saint Francis, would be rejected and martyred many times. Yes,
he had recognition in Europe, but how about food and clothing?

Benny was still wearing the suit made of material he had woven years before at the ashram of Gandhi. It was worn and shabby, and he still had only two pairs of socks and one pair of shoes. None of this really mattered to him much now, but he was tired of begging for the price of a piece of granite. Would he ever be able to buy a piece of porphyry? Would San Francisco open its heart and its purse to give him the tools and materials of his craft? Bufano wondered.

9 ' Everybody Gets a Piece of Benny

The constantly changing Manhattan skyline greeted Benny after his years of travel. Tall cathedrals of steel and concrete fired his imagination: "If steel and terra cotta can be used with such beauty architecturally, why can't they be used artistically?"

He stopped for a few days to see his family. Lucrecia killed the depression-lean fatted calf for this prodigal son, who had become a man of international importance in the art world. She boasted about Beniamino to her neighbors, showing them copies of the reviews her son had brought her, and with added pride bragged that he could speak French.

Canio read the reviews. Unimpressed, he asked what was the good of all this newspaper talk? It wouldn't make a millionaire out of Beniamino. It wouldn't even put spaghetti into his mouth.

Benny, now angry, replied that he was a famous man and his father should appreciate that. But Canio laughed at the thought that this little shrimp was a famous man. Bufano turned away from him with a heavy heart.

Lucrecia looked scornfully at her husband and reminded him of his own arrival in New York. It was not a triumphant one; no newspaper article acclaimed him. In fact, Canio had come as a refugee with a price on his head. Canio angrily stomped out of the room.

Lucrecia gave her son special care and tasty food. But this did not ease the hurt from his father. She pleaded with Beniamino to make his home in New York. She was getting old and so was Canio. She talked to him of getting a studio in the Village where all of his friends and family would be near him. But Beniamino was not to be dissuaded: he felt that he must get

114

back to San Francisco; that was his home now. He looked lovingly at his mother and felt sorry that he had to refuse her.

Although he knew he couldn't live near his father anymore, Bufano had qualms about going to San Francisco. It had become an ogre to him. Art, to Bufano, should create controversy — but not hatred, hostility and venom. And from what he had heard in Paris from some of his friends, San Francisco had become a hotbed of dissension about his art: the birds and other animals might have loved St. Francis, but Bufano's St. Francis, the city felt, was for the birds.

Upon arriving in San Francisco, the first thing Benny did was to contact Ansel Adams. Since Bufano's departure to Paris, Adams had opened a distinguished photographic gallery with a man named Joseph A. Danysh. Danysh knew many influential people, and Adams suggested to Bufano that they go to see him. After meeting Bufano and being apprised of his problems, Danysh said he would introduce him around. As they were discussing the problems of artists, a florid-faced, beetle-browned Western Union boy entered. Danysh told Bufano that this boy wrote the neatest short stories he'd ever read; he had the touch of genius in him, but nobody took him seriously. Danysh introduced the youth — Bill Saroyan! William Saroyan was as poor as Bufano; they became good friends.

The next morning Benny was on the corner of Montgomery and Market streets shouting, "Paper! Get your morning paper!" Bufano, darling of the artists' colony of Paris, had reverted to the days of his apprenticeship and was again selling papers for a living.

Over the years, Benny kept worrying about his St. Francis in the storehouse in Paris. He felt that the only way he could get sufficient money to bring back the statue would be to sell some of the works he had buried at Los Gatos on the estate of Colonel Wood. Benny was seething because he had heard that Wood had sold four or five of his pieces to a wealthy Mrs. Stern for $1500. He went to Mrs. Stern to find out about it. She said she had bought the pieces and was annoyed at Bufano for bothering her.

It was mid-July of 1931 when Bufano went to see The Old Gentleman. "I went down there with a friend of mine in a beaten-up truck. When I saw Wood I told him, 'I want to pick up my treasures. I'm dead broke and I've got to sell some of the stuff.'

"He looked innocent and said, 'Whoa now, Beniamino. Take it easy! I haven't got your stuff any more.'

"That made me furious. I shouted, 'What the hell are you talking about?'

"'Well . . . it's this way,' he said, trying to be calm. 'While you were in Europe, your wife and child were here and she pleaded with me to give her the stuff so she could sell it to support herself and the boy.'

"'Child!' I screamed. 'What child? What is this, long-distance insemination!?'

"Wood was plenty annoyed and said, 'I didn't even know you were married, much less that you had a child. I don't like people playing tricks on me. You lied to me years ago about that Texas trip. I gave you the money to study the cotton pickers. Instead, you got married!'

"'Hell,' I told him. 'I never really married her. It was a companionate marriage and we agreed I could leave whenever I felt like it.'

"'Well, it was real enough for you to have a kid,' he answered. 'She convinced me that you were her husband and the father of that child. And besides, she's going to sue you for a divorce and take every damn thing you have.'

"'Jeez,' I said, 'I didn't even know she had a kid.'

"The Old Man was mad as hops. 'How in hell did you expect her to get in touch with you? Nobody ever knows where the hell you are!'"

Stunned, Benny left the estate with his friend in that empty old broken-down truck.

Later, Benny told Danysh and Saroyan about his visit to Wood. "The Colonel had three chickens on the table for lunch, and we're starving to death! He says he hasn't paid Dreifuss because he's having trouble with the government because of his income tax. Hell, I wish I had an income tax to pay. So I asked the old geezer why he didn't give me the money he got from the sale of the things to Mrs. Stern. And you know what he did? He put his hand in his pocket and handed me fifty bucks. Just so he could ease his conscience, the old bastard. So you know what I did? I threw the money back at him and I said, 'Go buy a rope to hang yourself!' "

The two men were in complete sympathy with Bufano. Saroyan yelled that he wished to hell he knew the rich people Bufano knew. He wouldn't be sitting here in this dump. Benny pointed out that even if Saroyan had a million dollars he'd gamble it away.

Saroyan shrugged his shoulders. Only one thing was on his mind now — hunger. How about Benny making one of his "lousy" pizzas? (Saroyan admitted later it was the best pizza he ever tasted.) Pizzas were Bufano's specialty: they were cheap, easy to make, and filling. Sliding the cover off a battered breadbox, Benny pulled forth hard cheese, harder salami and some flour. Saroyan borrowed some tomato sauce from the grocery store next door, while Bufano prepared the dough. With everything ready, Benny ran almost a block to the kiln, which was still hot from firing the head of a St. Francis, to cook his pizza. It was cold and foggy outside, and Benny wore the *one* coat common to all three — Danysh, Bufano and Saroyan. ("That coat," Saroyan said years later, "was three times too big for any of us. It had been given to us by a friend of Leon Liebes, and the three of us shared it." Saroyan wrote a short story about the coat, which he said "is now lost to posterity." Danysh also mentioned later that the coat was "too big and baggy . . . but the problem in those days was not a matter of fashion fitness but of keeping warm.")

The following week Bufano wrote a letter to The Old Gentleman:

San Francisco, California
July 23, 1931

Dear Colonel Wood:

I believe that you will well understand that this letter is quite in place and that it is coming to you. It is, as you will see, in regard to my own creations that we mutually agreed to leave in the

safety of your care until I was able to possess a few dollars so as
to have a studio to put them in. Then, as you know, a portion of
them went to Paris under the protection of Mr. Verdier, for the
purpose of showing them in Paris. Among these pieces that Mr.
Verdier took to Paris were twelve pieces that belonged to you.
These twelve pieces were registered under your name as your
possessions. During the time that we gave the show at Verdier's
City of Paris, a department store, Mr. Cassasa made a list of all
the pieces that were exhibited there, including a full list of my
Chinese collection that were exhibited during the same time. Of
this list three copies were made; one copy went to you, one copy
was held for a record at the City of Paris, and the third is in my
possession. All this was done automatically in the business effi-
ciency of the City of Paris, and I am only recalling this to you
so that you may see clearly the truth of it all.

But what I really want to say is, that I left these things with
you as a friend, with all the simplicity and the faith of a child.
You will recall that we buried a portion of the things on your land
on the mountainside at Los Gatos, in secret silence between you
and me. I believe you will understand now that I find myself in a
very brutal position, silent and betrayed. I had hoped that at least
those things that we so joyfully buried were safe in hiding, away
from the hands of greedy, filthy merchants, but as you told me
the other day, they too had been ordered dug up and had joined
the sad fate of the others.

You, as a professional lawyer, might as well be reminded that
none of those things were done later than the date 1920. This
places the things in my own hands, their creator. They do not go
under the name of community law. Besides, seven of them are borrowed pieces. They do not belong to me. You cannot sell them,
you cannot will them to anyone, and I hold you responsible. I ask
justice, not charity.

It is only right to say that I have told you that I am in my
right place. No one has any right to interfere with the personal
affairs and the rights of others, and he who does this convicts
himself of blackmailing and murder in cold blood. Personal rights
are sacred in the silence only to those involved, and any gossip
in its regard is cowardly murder. Justice, not charity is the only
road to follow. This is the intolerant cry and voice of the Twen-
tieth Century.

This is all! With good wishes for your health.

In a letter to Bufano's attorney, Wood wrote:

I think we should never regret having tried to do a kindly act . . .
heal spiritual breaches. But you and I may, if we choose, forget
all about it. It is difficult for one to write of Benvenuto and not

seem bitter, revengeful, angry . . . yet it is not so. I do not hold him responsible any more than I would a rattlesnake, but we do not have to hug the rattlesnakes to our bosom, nor even endure them. Benvenuto to me, is a pathological specimen of humanity.

Bufano's lawyer later wrote to Colonel Wood in 1932, explaining Virginia's role in the whole affair:

> I believe that the recent difficulties are largely the result of your sympathy for his wife under the peculiar circumstances you recount, and particularly your assuming the responsibility of attempting to relieve her distress through the disposition of his things. If you had fully understood his attitude toward her, and her own peculiarities, you would probably have treated the matter differently. I assume that instruction in these matters continues to go forward, and that even in your case it may be said you "learned about women from her."

In speaking of this case, Bufano ended up by saying, "What kind of funny business was it that she named the kid Charles Erskine Scott Bufano? And how come she 'convinced' Wood to give her all my works of art, especially when Colonel Wood and I had secretly buried all my works so no crook could get them? These things I'll never understand."

Feeling hunted by what he called "the avaricious Virginia," Bufano tried desperately to collect his remaining works. Benny had gone to a museum in San Francisco that supposedly housed a large collection of his pieces, and when he found many works missing, he wrote to the director:

> I hate like the devil to blame Colonel Wood for any of the pieces missing, and it is for this reason that I would like to know just how many pieces you have at the Museum. According to my list, there are about twenty or thirty pieces missing. This number includes the seven or eight that I smashed up at the Legion. [Benny, unhappy with the experimental glazes he was working on, had smashed them in anger.] I am sorry that I made any trouble for you by doing it, but I am quite sure that you understand my feeling in the matter.
>
> I should like to bury all of the pieces that you have of mine, so as to get them out of your way, and particularly to release the temptation of another exhibition.

By now Bufano's old friend, Leopold Dreifuss (who had helped him during the Da Vinci School difficulties) had assumed

the $875 indebtedness to the Keystone Company and conse-
quently had sued Colonel Wood. Wood's deposition, at the time
of the trial, stated that in 1930 the Keystone Commercial Company had assigned the "judgment to Leopold Dreifuss who, in
turn had sued Bufano and obtained a judgment against him
in the sum of $692.15 principal, $436.05 interest and $8.25 costs."
Over the years the indebtedness had almost doubled itself! Of
course Bufano, a renowned bankrupt, never could pay this sum.
Not only was he broke, but his works had been taken; so he
couldn't raise the money by selling them. Benny, the hunted,
was trapped.

On November 24, 1931, Virginia obtained a divorce. An agreement was signed stating:

> The wife shall not claim any alimony for the support of herself
> in said suit against the husband . . . and it is agreed that the hus-
> band agrees to and does hereby sell, assign, transfer, set over and
> deliver unto the wife . . . the personal property itemized and set
> forth in the document attached hereto marked Exhibit "A", war-
> ranting full and complete title hereto. The wife, in turn, agrees to
> and does herewith forego and waive any claim for support, or ali-
> mony, or maintenance for herself, or attorney's fees in said divorce
> suit. . . . Further, the wife does release the husband from the obli-
> gation to support the minor child of the husband and the wife
> for the divorce period of one year and the date hereof.

Bufano lost most of his works of art to Virginia. "It was the worst
thing that could ever happen to an artist. I almost died."

Later, in an article in the *Oakland Tribune*, Virginia gave her
side of her life with Bufano:

> I divorced Bufano to give back to him something I had taken
> away . . . that was his free spirit . . . the freedom of a mind that
> combines the virtues and tragedies of both a child and a genius.
> He was not designed for domestic life. I would not hold him. I
> have cast my own life into the background for him and my one
> regret is that in his freedom he does not know his son, a child
> who gives promise of becoming an artist as great as his father.

Poverty was not new to Bufano and the depression was simply
something he had always lived with. The only time his family
had been comfortable was in San Fele, when Canio had held a
position in the city government, but Beniamino had been too

young to remember anything of that time except what Lucrecia
had told him. By 1933 the depression was in full swing: there
had been four long years of poverty, frustration and disappointment for Bufano. "I was really up shit creek in 1933," he recalled. "If it hadn't been for my good friend, Leon Liebes, I'd
have died of hunger."

He was referring to an agreement, dated September 25, 1933,
between himself, Leon Liebes and Harry Camp. This agreement
stated that Benny was an artist, "who, because of the depressed
conditions of the times and to certain domestic and personal difficulties is considerably in debt and entirely without funds, and
has remaining to him only a very few of his artistic productions."
Liebes and Camp, "moved by a desire to assist him" during this
difficult period, and also by a "high regard for his artistic work
and a desire to own and possess such of them as he may execute
during the existence of this contract, agree to pay Bufano $200
monthly for twelve months." Bufano also agreed to sell "certain
of his completed works of art" to Liebes so that the agreement
could be extended "for a fixed term of three years." For the sale
of his works, Bufano was to receive an additional $1000 "for re-
finishing and repairing his studio."

As usual, something went wrong with this contract and Benny
was flat broke again. Whether he signed a contract or not, Bufano
never seemed to feel that he was bound by it. Blithely, and often
tragically, he swam the sea of life with contracts flooding after
him. Sometimes they caught up with him and a jail would take
him to its breast.

He rented the old stable garage of the Holladay House, high
on the hill of Lafayette Square, but there is no evidence that
he ever paid the $16-a-month rent. Here in this studio he set
himself up with a rickety old cot for a bed and an oil drum
with a chimney for a heater and stove. Bufano's closest friends
at the time were Bill Saroyan, Joe Danysh and the young Will
Rogers.

"We didn't have a pot to pee in, so we mooched dinners wherever we could. Rogers was the only one around who had a few
bucks, so he was the one who paid most of the time. In a pinch,

we used to pilfer a can of coffee, a bottle of wine or a loaf of bread from the neighboring grocery stores to help fill us up.

"Saroyan always said this was a hell of a time to be living in. No work, no women, no nothing. Nothing but W.P.A.

" 'Hell,' I told him, 'so I'll go on W.P.A. Joe Danysh [then with the W.P.A.] can get me on the artists' project.' Saroyan said they'd never catch him going on charity. He was a proud devil. So I jokingly told him he was an Armenian son-of-a-bitch. 'You'd rather die of hunger than ask for anything. W.P.A. isn't charity. The government is the people and if the people are hungry they're entitled to take their own money from the government.'

" 'Okay,' said Saroyan, 'you do it, and I'll borrow from you!' "

The next day Bufano stood in line at the intake department of the W.P.A. office. "The ninety bucks I got took care of us. When I was hungry I used to take a pot of oatmeal to Sausalito where I went sketching. I never forgot to take along a fistful of salt to calm down a cow and milk her directly into the pot of mush."

Now that Benny was on the art project of the W.P.A. he had an assured income and a ready source of materials. But he wanted to experiment in a new medium that the W.P.A. did not provide: granite was not hard enough for Benny; it had to be stainless steel! Benny wrote letters to the steel industry, and the Columbia Steel Company responded by sending him several sheets of this material.

Bufano's small frame was covered with strong muscles. He decided not to cast the steel in molds but to pound and hammer it cold directly into the shapes he wanted. The steel resisted him. He set his jaw, gritted his teeth and squinted his small blue eyes as he pounded. Suddenly his hammer broke under the heavy pounding! He picked up another; it broke too. He threw it down and took another. Slowly, inexorably, the steel began to change its shape. Benny worked on, far, far into the night. He was so engrossed in his pounding that it was a long time before he became conscious of a rival pounding on the door of his studio. He put down his hammer and nearly collapsed with the pain of his tensed muscles, which cramped and refused to relax. He staggered to the door and opened it. An angry crowd of indignant Italian neighbors stood there in their night shirts.

Bufano used an Italian accent to tell of the anger of his neighbors. "What's-a-the matter, you son-of-a-bitch, Benny! You pound and pound. We no can sleep. You no got no sense? If you no cut it out we call the police!"

"It's-a two o'clock in the morning, you bum!" one man yelled.

Benny apologized; "I'm sorry, fellows. I didn't realize what time it was."

Grumbling, the men left.

He looked at the bent steel. "Now, what have you got to say, you stubborn bastard! Who's stronger — you or me?"

Bufano, the incurable optimist, rarely gave up an idea once it was born. Remembering his plan for the *St. Francis de la Varenne*, still in storage in Paris, he now saw such a project within the realm of possibility. W.P.A. would be paying for all of his statues and could provide the materials under the artists' project. He would create a masterpiece, an enormous stainless-steel statue of St. Francis to stand atop Twin Peaks, overlooking San Francisco. He discussed his idea with Joe Danysh, who had become regional director of the W.P.A. art projects. Danysh was all for it, recommended it and got the okay for it. Benny started work on the eight-foot-high model of redwood and copper for the projected 180-foot statue. This great work was to stand higher than the Statue of Liberty (which Benny regarded as "a pretty poor piece of work").

All hell broke loose when Benny presented this model to the San Francisco Art Commission, which had to approve the design. Pictures of Benny and his model filled the front pages of the newspapers. Vicious attacks were mixed with words of praise. But Benny didn't care what they said. Just so long as they said something! The eight-foot model stood peacefully, waiting for the final decision of the experts — the church, the politicians, the artists and the common citizens of San Francisco. It stood in a small committee room of the Art Commission for years, unconscious of the winds of controversy blowing about its gentle, saintly head.

Columnist Westbrook Pegler called Benny's proposed statue a "tombstone-cutter's nightmare! It is a figure with the conventionalized head of the 1910 model of a family doctor, with a pointed beard, enclosed in an aviator's helmet and having beneath the chin a sort of bib, or drool cloth! The hands are upraised in the standard posture of the guest of honor at a stickup, and the figure then declines, round, rigid as a concrete pipe and innocent of fold or human line, to the waist, where it disappears into a barrel extending to the base."

Reading this diatribe, Benny laughed heartily. "As long as Pegler doesn't ignore me, I'm not worried."

Pegler offered to wager $200 that he could take an ordinary beer mallet, a carpenter's chisel and a plain rock and make a better St. Francis than Bufano's. The San Francisco Press Club covered the bet for Benny, who presented Pegler with the tools for hammering and chiseling and a piece of granite from which to carve his work of art. Pegler contemptuously refused to use the tools but instead went to work with a bung starter and a wad of mud. He created an atrocity, which he sent to the Press Club, and conceded the controversy, insisting he was ill and had a bad back. Bufano collected the $200 and gave scholarships to two young, poverty-stricken artists. Later, he and Pegler became friends and had many a good laugh over the incident.

The controversy over the statue went on for years, culminating finally in a tumultuous meeting of the Art Commission on February 3, 1937. The room was filled "with a motley throng of bushy-haired, bearded, shabbily dressed, vociferously gesticulating and shouting artists, press men and cameras, citizens yelling out their opinions in loud and uninhibited voices, priests, draped in black suits and reversed collars, looking dignified but determined, and opposition members of the Art Commission who were attempting to block the project by initiating an open competition for the work." The newspapers had a field day telling the story of Bufano's St. Francis.

Gertrude Atherton and other women verbally attacked the statue: "Hideous! . . . that wooden thing . . . it looks like a hold-up! Grotesque! . . ."

Bufano tore his hair in wild despair. "It was these women who were perpetrating a holdup! They were trying to hold up work on my statue! That's just like women! They're nothing but a bunch of bitches!"

Otis Oldfield, the well-known painter, stood up and spoke: "San Francisco is satisfied with such atrocities as the rah-rah statue of Marshall at Mason and Market Streets, and that angel-on-a-ball in Union Square, nothing but photographic taxidermy in stone. The trouble is, most people are used to the objective art of the Victorian Period. Benny's statue is subjective art. It is the crystallization of a great emotion, not a copy of a portrait!"

Artist Matthew Barnes added: "That statue of St. Francis will do more for San Francisco than anything else has. If people can't see the stupendousness of it, it's just too bad. Bufano has put his whole soul into it. Put the statue up on Twin Peaks and the city will learn to love it!"

Benny applauded with his friends in the audience.

Joseph Danysh, in presenting a petition signed by 147 prominent local artists asking the Art Commission to accept Bufano's statue, said: "Heretofore, lack of professional artists' opinions has been one of the reasons for the disapproval of the statue. The project will give employment to many needy artists and it should be put through. Few American sculptors have either the background or the ability to make such a gigantic statue, and Bufano is the only sculptor working directly in the new medium, stainless steel, the medium decided upon because of its durability. It is not fair to judge a gigantic statue to be erected on top of a hill, from a small model carved out of wood."

Father George of the Franciscan Order blurted out: "This work is not artistic. It disgraces our Order and it disgraces Saint Francis. It is a monstrosity." To this, John J. Mitty, the Catholic archbishop of San Francisco, responded: "I am delighted with the statue. It will be a tremendous asset to the city and will become one of the most distinctive and outstanding monuments throughout the world!" Some of the crowd yelled, some hooted, and some applauded the archbishop!

Artist Ray Boynton wrote a letter defending Bufano's statue:

It is daring and it is unique and it is imaginative. It has the purity
that distinguishes great art . . . from everything else. The whole
conception is a challenge to generations of people after we are
dead. It is probably the most original conception of St. Francis
since Giotto's frescoes. It is uniquely modern in its material and
execution and timeless in its form. No one else in this country
could conceive and execute it.

Bufano's eyes were filled with tears when the letter was read at
the meeting.

The mural artist Frank Bergman spoke: "I'd hate to see a
statue on or near Twin Peaks . . . either Bufano's or anyone else's.
Putting statuary on elevated spots is a strange human weakness.
A hill top should be crowned (if it has to be crowned) only with
truly monumental architecture. I object to Saints . . . Bufano's
or anyone else's. To have a symbol of love looking down upon
our 'man-eat-man' civilization with so many of our neighbors
hungry, would be the meanest irony and hypocrisy. I mean this
in the wider sense, and not as a reflection against one individual.
Wise old Colonel Wood once said, 'Christianity has never been
practiced.' Please let's forget all the Saints."

Dr. Jason Nobel Pierce, pastor of the First Congregational
Church and president of the San Francisco Federation of
Churches, gave his opinion: "A statue of peace like this of St.
Francis would be eminently fitting. I advocate its erection, as
soon as possible, on a suitable elevated spot. St. Francis, especially as conceived by Bufano, has nothing to do with Catholicism. He belongs to the whole world."

One minister criticized the model saying: "Saint Francis was
a man of poverty and humbleness. Why does not Mr. Bufano's
statue have patches on his robes?"

Benny replied indignantly, "I am a sculptor, not a tailor."
The crowd roared. "A man in patches would be a botch! I am
perfectly willing to make reasonable changes, but, naturally, I
cannot make enough alterations to suit everybody here."

At this, a bearded artist in the crowd yelled, "To hell with
them, Benny! The people of San Francisco don't deserve a work

of art! They'd better put up a scarecrow on the top of that crazy hill. Maybe that would suit everybody!"

The Art Commission approved the statue and Benny was carried out on the shoulders of the triumphant artists. They proceeded to a small coffeehouse where the celebration was continued until the wee hours of the morning.

On his way back to his studio, Benny was stopped by two thugs who pulled a gun and demanded his money. Benny grinned at them as he held his hands aloft, just like his St. Francis. "This is symbolic," he said. "Take what I've got boys. You're welcome to all of it." The thugs frisked his pockets and found 47 cents. They went off disgusted, yet with puzzled looks on their faces. Benny heard one say to the other, "What the hell did that little shrimp mean? Symbolic!"

Yes, it was symbolic. Bufano, with his hands in the air, was unconsciously thinking of himself as St. Francis with his hands uplifted, overlooking the great San Francisco Bay, pitying the people of the world for their lack of understanding and blessing them for their greatness.

10 ⸀ Benny at Work

Bufano's new St. Francis was to have no easier life than the one that was reclining in the Paris warehouse. Immediately after the statue received the approval of the Art Commission, a violent clamor arose over the estimated cost of its upkeep. The Park Commission disclaimed the responsibility, maintaining that to keep the stainless-steel and copper monument bright and shining would cost about $10,000 a year.

A question also was raised about the desirability of using stainless steel as an art medium. A letter from the Allegheny Steel Company to the *San Francisco Chronicle* on February 12, 1937, stated:

> Without reference to the artistic merits of the Bufano creation, but with reference solely to stainless steel as a material for art and architectural work, such an implication is unfair to this material which is a versatile medium, and has enormous possibilities for artistic and architectural expression.
>
> Far from being a "cheap" material, stainless steel is the finest of the commercial metals of alloys, and is not infrequently referred to as "popular priced platinum." Its possibilities for the artist and the architect are just beginning to be realized.
>
> The medium, moreover, embodies the essentials and provides a versatile range of possibilities, from finest detail to utmost simplicity, for the exercise of the creative ability of the artist and the skill of the craftsman.
>
> This stainless steel statue of the medieval saint will be almost impervious to time or the elements; the stainless steel will be made of a new alloy, containing two per cent of white glass, in addition to its iron, chromium, carbon and manganese content.

Although the Park Commission still refused to take the responsibility of keeping the statue shining, it did set aside $9000 for the irrigation of the mountain St. Francis would beautify and agreed to care for it so that it should be green with natural verdure throughout the year.

Nothing happened. Despite the approval, St. Francis got the run-around; he was conveniently forgotten in the maze of city politics. However, Bufano didn't forget. He would keep reminding the politicians for years to come about his St. Francis.

When asked what happened to the models for the statue, Benny answered, "I made a number of models . . . about seven . . . three in wood. One was placed in the Stanford Museum, another at the museum in Santa Clara . . . that was a loan, two or three are with friends of mine, and I have two in my studio." When asked what happened to another plan, that of placing his St. Francis on Telegraph Hill in San Francisco, Benny became bitter and criticized the politics of the city for the breakdown in the arrangements for his statue.

Meanwhile he worked on animals. He had developed a philosophy and a love of animals from his travels in India and his love for St. Francis. He produced a sleek-backed bear, a bear with two cubs, and a bear with the Madonna, a seal, a frog, a mouse, penguins, a barracuda, a walrus, birds, horses, cows, and a cat. He never created a dog, except for the one from his medallion period. About his animal group Bufano remarked, "Take the bear, for example. Some people think of a bear as a bear. I am concerned with the bear only in form. The bear was designed as it is to carry out the canonic qualities of determination and strength."

No work of Bufano's ever shows cruelty or meanness or the strident in nature. It took years for his experiences with nature to materialize, but when he had the chance, his nature studies exploded.

What can be more sleek than Bufano's cat? In many ways it doesn't look like a cat, but as he would say, it's not supposed to. All it needs is the feline grace of a cat, the general qualities of a cat, to be a cat. In Bufano's world it is so much like a cat that one can hear it purr. What makes him particularly happy is that his animals invite children to play on them. Children love to run their hands over smooth surfaces, they love peace and quiet; they don't want rough, hard surfaces to rip their tender skin, neither do they want to play on something that might get broken or damaged. Bufano's animals are made for the people to enjoy, to sit on if they want, to slide down, to crawl up, but they never have to worry about scuffing or scraping the material. "Nothing pleases me more than to see the children of God . . . humans and animals . . . play together."

Of all the letters Bufano received, he treasured one above all the rest. It is from a little girl named Glenn Ahearn who, after seeing and playing with his animals on display at the San Francisco Civic Center, wrote him:

> Dear Mr. Bufano
>
> I love your statues and I like the mouse best of all. My brother likes the cat best of all. When we left I kissed the mouse goodbye. I am a girl.
>
> Glenn Ahearn

To Bufano, a work of art should stimulate people as his statues stimulated that child. For an artist there is no greater satisfaction in the world than to see his work appreciated. But it is not necessary for anyone to show his appreciation of the esthetic qualities of Bufano's work; all that is essential is that the person just rub his hands over the smoothness of the work. "It should be inviting to the touch as well as to the eyes." Benny felt it was too bad people are denied this pleasure in museums. The sense of touch has been vastly important to his art; perhaps this is one of the reasons why the Braille Institute asked Bufano to lecture to blind artists on the importance of touch to the artist.

For him, perhaps the most beautifully designed animal is the seal or the porpoise. If you look at the lines on his beautiful seal, you see it is a statue of poetry in static motion. It is ready to dive, to flip through the air, yet it does not, cannot move. This is Bufano's genius: the capturing of life and action while at rest. So it is with the wading bird done in red porferino, and the mouse in black granite. All his animals are quiet, peaceful, yet they breathe life; to the thousands of children who have seen them, and to the artist himself, his animals have a soul.

Of Bufano's animal sculptures critic Sam Fusco said:

Bufano's attempt in this field is an ancient art subtly revived in a new medium, tempered with the inspired docility which the affectionate St. Francis imbued in his love for animals. This little world of animals is the dream of the child at bed time, whose mind is filled with the fanciful images of the animals in his fairy mood, the memory of the equestrians at the circus, and the picturesque beasts raised from stories of the African veldt. A child's thought needs only a few suggestions to build in his mind the picture of a growling tiger and this Bufano has done with his inimitable few planes and lines, like the necromancy of the magician's silk hat from which pops a cuddling rabbit. The crab looks horrible with so many ugly claws. We would like it better if it were not so terrible. So Bufano makes it look smooth and friendly and why shouldn't the frog raise its head high if it chooses to appear strong and defiant?

Benny did one, *The Toothless Bear and the Virgin*, which Fusco described as having "the reassuring feminine face of the Virgin placed at the paws of the snarling bear to show that it is really harmless and cannot hurt anyone."

In 1945, long after *The Bear and the Virgin* was created, Professor Eugene Neuhaus of the University of California wrote in the *Saturday Evening Post* of January 25th about another bear:

It may be an aesthetic triumph but it is no bear. It has for example, only four teeth. It has no eyes. It is without a tongue. It has the tail of a beaver and the torso of a seal. And the—er—animal is utterly undynamic. This is certainly not a California bear. Perhaps it is a Malayan sun bear.

Detail in these figures is not apparent for the reason that a snarling saliva-dripping fang would hardly be suggestive of gentleness and since the most brutal of carnivori have an element of calm and quiet, the sculptor, through the elimination of detail, has created a style that interprets the docile moments of the animal's character. These works are exemplary in the sense that they reflect Benny's fundamentals that a true likeness in a reproductive medium cannot possibly exist, and the only reproduction that can be tolerated as being an absolute sincerity is the lineal aspect of a structural form.

Bufano's W.P.A. group of animals is in a playful mood — yet serious. He treats with the character of animals as brought to us through folk lore and legendary myths. In our early reading we learned that children were taught that animals were brave, gentle and playful. As children, we realized the friendly aspect of animals and thoroughly appreciated their docility. But with maturity, we took on another aspect which advised us to destroy animals whose habits were annoying to the economic well-being of a community.

Bufano was diverted from his animals by the City of Portland, Oregon, formerly the home of Charles Erskine Scott Wood. The people of the city wanted to have a memorial raised to Wood as a great patron of the arts. Bufano, who had been a close friend of the colonel's since about 1919, was the natural choice for this work, which was commissioned in 1935. An article in the *American Mercury* refers to this:

> Benny designed a symbol of purity and called it "Childhood," but Portland's pietistical city fathers insisted that it be given more clothing. Refusing to impeach his lofty intent, Benny reclaimed the statue, and it now stands in Colonel Wood's home town of Los Gatos. As usual, Benny got nothing but kudos.
>
> The sparse attire of "Childhood" was consistent with Benny's own indifference to dress. When he carves the human figure, he exercises the utmost economy in raiment.

At the time, Bufano had little to say about the rejection of his undraped child's figure. He dismissed its critics by calling them "petty little people. Do they seek to smother art because of their own animality?"

These and many other minor rejections irked him, but they did not get him down. Nothing could discourage him since he had become imbued with the idea of immortalizing Sun Yat-sen in stainless steel and granite, but he had to wait for the proper time; he had to get money. And now that he was on the W.P.A., things were beginning to shape up.

While waiting for the go-ahead on the St. Francis, Benny wangled a commission from the W.P.A. to do a commemorative statue of Sun Yat-sen. The statue was to be presented to the city by the Kuomintang and the W.P.A. art project, which was financing the work. By using steel, Bufano saved the W.P.A. a great deal of money. If the statue were cast in the usual materials, the work would cost $25,000; working directly with the steel, Bufano reduced the expense of the materials to about $500.

"We know you did it, Benny. . . . We saw you . . . but we still don't believe it!" said one of the Columbia Steel Company's production executives to Bufano, as he watched him working in his studio on the statue of the Chinese revolutionary. Bufano hand-beat the metal into symmetrical forms, first gluing newspaper over the sheet metal to protect the surface from scars as he worked. Stainless steel cannot be annealed and must be shaped without heat, since disturbance of the molecular structure reduces it to ordinary iron. Bufano had to pound it cold. The steel men had told him it was impossible.

"Nothing is impossible, not even the impossible." That was Bufano's answer.

They wanted to know what the newspaper was for. "I told them the glue and the paper protected the metal from pitting. It was a primitive way of doing it but it worked." They suggested that perhaps they could work out a formula for the glue in their laboratories. Bufano said that was not necessary: he had bought the glue in the five-and-ten and it worked perfectly. When he showed them the steel under the paper, it was not pitted.

The statue stood fourteen feet high. The head and hands were carved of red granite, the body and arms beaten out of stainless steel. Bufano had to supply his own tools because he couldn't use the usual wooden tools the W.P.A. supplied. Cannon balls and bowling balls served as bases around which to work the metal. After he had beaten them into the shapes he wanted, Benny joined the various parts by electric welding. He became a good welder.

The executives of the steel company told Benny that if he ever wanted a welding job they would give him one any time. Bufano thanked them, but he was thinking of when he had worked at welding iron in a smithy because his father insisted that he get a regular job, where he could learn a trade, instead of "fooling around" with artists.

"I was about fourteen years old and my father was having a hell of a time earning a living for that big family. Everybody worked at whatever jobs they could find. I was an apprentice for Herbert Adams, who was the founder of the National Sculpture Society, and this didn't pay much. One night I got home to find my father quarreling with my mother, saying that I was a lazy good-for-nothing and ought to take a job where I could help my family. As I came in my mother began pleading with me.

" 'Please, Beniamino,' she implored. 'Do what Papa say. Maybe he's-a-right. It's hard make living with sculpture. You do what your Papa say. He love you and he no want you to be poor like us. Please, Beniamino.' "

Bufano's voice always went soft when he spoke of his mother: "I couldn't resist her pleading eyes so I went to work for Martinelli, a friend of my father's who had a blacksmith shop. At first I was resentful, but soon I found the work interesting and challenging. And then I began hating my work again. In my fifth week I picked up a piece of steel that I was supposed to weld to another piece. When it was red hot I began hammering it to the other piece. I pounded and pounded, but nothing happened. Harder! Harder! Then the head of the heavy hammer broke off and smashed through a window. I stared about as though awakened from a dream.

"Joe Martinelli yelled, 'What the hell happened?'

"I told him I was sorry but I couldn't work for him any more. 'I guess I have to be an artist,' I said. I picked up my lunch sack and started out of the shop. I crossed Fifth Avenue and ran through the small alley where I found myself staring into the studio of Martiny, my former employer. Tears rolled down my face when I saw a young man of eighteen or nineteen cleaning the studio, doing exactly the same work that I used to do. No chance for me. Just then I heard a kind voice behind me. It was Martiny. He wanted to know where I had been keeping myself.

"I told him I'd been doing lots of things in Pennsylvania and that I had learned a lot. I guessed I'd be a prize fighter like my brother Tony. I said this to get a rise out of Martiny. He told me I was a damned fool and asked me into the studio. 'I need a job,' I told him and then told him of my experience as a welder. He wanted to know if I had met James Fraser, the great sculptor who made the wonderful Indian statue called the *End of the Trail*.

" 'Hell, I know all the artists in the Village, great or small.' We went over to see Fraser.

"When we entered his studio, Fraser was sculpting a group of Mrs. Whitney and her children. Fraser stopped his work and greeted us and then stared at me for a few minutes. He asked if I was the boy who used to work for Herbert Adams. Martiny said I was the boy, but Adams had written that he was staying on in Europe indefinitely, and there would be no more work for me. Martiny wondered if Fraser could find a place for me. When Fraser said he thought he could, I asked him if I could start right away. Fraser and Martiny both laughed because I was such an eager beaver.

" 'Before I get started, Mr. Fraser, I better tell you that I've got a problem.'

"Fraser wanted to know who didn't.

"What I mean is that I quit my mechanic's job because I wanted to be an artist, but my father threatened to murder me if I quit. I'm afraid to go home. Could I sleep in the studio until things blow over at home?'

"Fraser said all artists go through the same thing. He went through practically the same thing when he was a kid and he told me to go ahead and make myself at home; I could sleep on the floor. I hated to have my mother worry about me, but I didn't dare go home to tell her where I was. Martiny said he'd drop by and tell her where I was so she wouldn't worry."

Lucrecia had visited her son briefly during the next three days and told him how Canio was taking his departure: every night when Canio returned home he'd look about expectantly, hoping to see Benny. "He come home, Lucrecia? Beniamino come home?" Canio had asked her.

"No, Canio. He no come home. You drive him away. You hit him. You yell at him. He's old enough now. He know what he want."

"He quit job with Joe. He break his promise. He break Joe's window. He break our hearts. I don't want him to be poor like us."

"He don't care if he be poor. He wants to be an artist."

"He turn out big bum like all artists. No wanna work. It's
your fault if he turn out big bum." Canio looked at her suspiciously. "You know where he is?"

"No, I know nothin'. He never be bum. He not lazy, my
Beniamino. Sculpture work hard work."

"Sure it's hard work, but you get nothin' for it."

Each night the conversation went the same way. As the first
week of Benny's disappearance came to a close, Lucrecia became
worried about Canio. The night before, she had been awakened
by strange noises, and when she gained her senses she realized
that Canio had been sobbing and moaning. She woke him up
and Canio continued his crying, as if in a nightmare.

"Maybe he get killed," he sobbed. "Maybe something terrible
happen to him. Why I be so mean to him?" He sobbed against
Lucrecia's bosom.

"Don't cry, Canio. It's all right now. I found Beniamino today.
He no get killed."

"Where is he?" Canio jumped out of bed. "I go. I bring him
home."

"You crazy, Canio. He all right. He in Fraser's studio in
MacDougal Alley. You go to sleep and he come home tomorrow."

Canio grabbed his pants and shirt, pulled them on, stepped
into his shoes and ran down to the Alley. Fraser never locked
the door of his studio, so Canio entered. There, in the dim light
from the street lamp, Canio saw a small bundle, curled up and
fast asleep on the floor. Canio kneeled and shook the bundle.
"Beniamino! Beniamino!" he whispered. Benny stirred, then sat
up. His father grabbed him and held him close. He kissed him on
both cheeks. "My Beniamino! You come home with Papa! You
be artist if you want. I no bawl you out no more. You be artist."

How far away were those days with his father and mother,
his work as a welder and then with Fraser. He was now famous
but still so poor he had to go on W.P.A. to earn a living. In this,
Canio was right. Bufano wondered if he'd ever earn a living
from his art.

Now the statue of Sun Yat-sen was to be unveiled and Bufano was proud because of the honors bestowed upon him. At

the dedication on November 11, 1937, an address by Hon. Victor K. Kwong, of the Kuomintang government of China in America, said in part:

> And as a fitting memorial to Dr. Sun, this monument is truly a magnificent work of art. Bufano, the gifted artist to whom we are indebted and who lived and worked with Dr. Sun during the Chinese Revolution, has caught the spirit of the distinguished Chinese leader. It is at once simple and dignified and is an eloquent embodiment of Dr. Sun's greatness and the high plane of Chinese civilization. This greatness transcends mere national limits and Dr. Sun is acclaimed as one of the world's great men. As you can see, the figure is garbed in the formal Chinese attire of long gown and vest, with the hands holding a cane. Its proportions are twice life-size.

At the dedication ceremonies it was said that the monument was sponsored by the S.F. Park Commission with materials furnished by the Kuomintang supporters in America.

> It is fourteen feet high and stands on a seven foot base of reinforced concrete, surfaced with a red terrazza of the same color as the head and hands, which are of polished granite. The body is constructed of sheets of stainless steel shaped cold, riveted together with stainless steel rivets, the seams being welded with an electric arc using stainless steel electrodes. It is believed to be as permanent as any known sculptural medium. This is the first time that stainless steel has been used in monumental sculpture and the first time that any sculptor has combined stone and metal in a public monument.

Later, in a letter to a friend in the Washington office of the W.P.A., Bufano wrote about the unveiling.

> I was delighted to receive your telegram! The dedication went off beautifully. There were many thousands who witnessed the dedication. It was held in Saint Mary's Square . . . to my surprise, everybody seems to be very enthusiastic about the statue. And also, to my disappointment, there were no adverse criticisms on the thing at all. Not that I don't like it, but I was just surprised, that's all!

> Nearly the whole day was devoted to the dedication and we had some very beautiful editorials on the statue. A week later the Chinese gave a dinner, with over one hundred and fifty people attending, both Chinese and outsiders. It was a surprise party for me, and at this party the Chinese awarded me the Order of the Jade. I was a little bit surprised and naturally, glad to get it.

11 ⸱ Miss Peace,
the Unfashionable Nun

Bufano was still on W.P.A. when the San Francisco papers came out with the news that the Golden Gate International Exposition was being planned for 1939. Always on the alert for a commission, Benny had no sooner read this than he rushed to the exposition headquarters. Benny already had a plan for two groups of three figures, one of them a statue of Peace, for the exposition. Unlike the disappointing 1915 exposition, this time he came away with a contract; he'd be paid $2500 for this work! One fly in the ointment of his elation, however, was the limitation on size: knowing his love of colossal statues, the officials had included a clause limiting the height of the works to five feet, barely the size of Benny. This was frustrating for a sculptor who liked to look up at his statues.

Nevertheless, he was jubilant. With this money added to his W.P.A. salary he would be nothing less than a millionaire! Enthusiastically he started work. Nothing could stop him now. But the limitation on height was ridiculous. He might compensate by keeping some of his work at five feet, but Peace? Never! Peace would have to be a minimum of fifty feet — a hundred feet — even five hundred feet would be better!

"Don't be a fool. They'll break the contract!" a friend warned. Bufano finally settled for thirty feet. He borrowed money to buy two tons of stainless steel and a block of granite, and started chipping and hammering.

After working for a month, he asked for his installment of $625, "which was due three weeks ago." Suddenly Leopold Dreifuss, who had always kept an eagle eye on Benny's activities,

138

learned that his victim was about to come into money and swooped down upon his prey. Dreifuss sent the sheriff after Benny. The amount of Benny's indebtedness had sky-rocketed from $664.55 to $1,596.92.

"This Dreifuss! Damn him!"

For several months the case dragged on with letters, recriminations and charges between Benny, Colonel Wood, who had promised to pay the debt, and Dreifuss, who held the note. Finally Dreifuss, weary of it all, had his attorneys contact the exposition people. He said, through his lawyers, that he would now settle everything for $750 and asked the exposition to pay Benny promptly. The exposition company said it could not release "any payments to Mr. Bufano . . . until he secures a release from the Sheriff's office . . ." Benny borrowed $750 from a friend, paid off Dreifuss and received $937.50 from the exposition company out of which he paid back the $750 to his friend.

The exposition ran into financial trouble about this time and Benny was asked to finish *Peace* in plaster. He refused! They cancelled his commission and he was stuck with $7000 worth of materials that took him twelve years to pay off. "It wouldn't have been so bad," said Bufano, "but I had to keep the statue in storage and that always costs money."

He had no Madame Rosalie to speak for him now. His St. Francis was still lying in a Paris warehouse and Bufano was sure that the thrifty Frenchman was keeping a careful account of the cost of storage, Rosalie notwithstanding. He shuddered to think of this ever-increasing debt. Now again a statue, his *Peace*, would be lying in storage accumulating more indebtedness for its maker.

Later, Japanese-Americans became interested in *Peace* and promised to pay Bufano for his work and the statue. They tried to raise some money, but before raising the full amount they presented the statue to Mayor Angelo Rossi, as a gift to the city. Then came Pearl Harbor. The Japanese-Americans were ordered off to detention camps, but before they left, a small group visited Benny.

"Here's five hundred dollars, Mr. Bufano. It was all we could raise."

"No," said Benny, pushing the money back into their hands. "Keep it. You need the money more than I do. I'll take care of the statue."

So, the statue of Peace became an orphan again. A sad disarticulated orphan, its stone head in one place, its stainless-steel body in another part of the warehouse. No one in the city could decide where it should be placed. Some people conveniently forgot they had ever heard of, or ever promised anything about the statue. "At least I got rid of Dreifuss!" Benny said philosophically. He blessed himself sacrilegiously, saying, "Amen to mayhem!"

With the war on, *Peace* rested in a warehouse.

After the war he tried to get various countries interested in his statue of *Peace*, but all efforts failed. Eventually, in 1953, the storage company put Benny's *Peace* up for auction. Things looked bad until Benny's old friends, the newspapermen, came to his aid. The *San Francisco Chronicle* purchased the statue. As the *Chronicle* said:

> Beniamino Bufano's majestic granite and stainless steel statue of "Peace" has been purchased by the Chronicle for eventual presentation to the city of San Francisco. The sale forestalled a public auction that had been scheduled for today because Bufano could not afford to pay a $750 storage bill on the statue.
>
> The twelve ton, thirty foot figure of a benign and compassionate woman had lain in a water front warehouse for more than ten years, and when the public sale was announced last week several stores and commercial interests made plans to buy it. The Chronicle's purchase made it certain that the statue will be located for the benefit of the entire city, and not be used for commercial purposes.
>
> Bufano worked for nearly two years on it, chiseling and polishing the simple, flowing lines of the figure's cowled head and shoulders out of a single massive block of California black granite. The stainless steel head piece is fashioned into a towering base forming the flowing, almost ecclesiastical robes of the woman. The steel base, more or less cylindrical in shape, towers some twenty-two feet high; the granite head and shoulders rise above it another seven and a half feet.

Benny said that he "sculptured *Peace* in the form of a projectile to express the idea that if peace is to be preserved today it must be an enforced peace . . . enforced by the democracies against fascist barbarism. Modern warfare, which involves the bombing of innocent women and children, has destroyed the concept of a peace with the conventional motif of olive branches and doves. *Peace* is one of my finest works. The simplified head could belong to any race."

Bufano constantly referred to the symbolism involved in any of his works, and, although he pretended to be an atheist, he prayed to God or to some god. He said, "If peace does not come to the sick world it will not be because I have not prayed. It may be because God is deaf. Deaf to the sense of His own creation that made Jesus utter in despair, 'My God, my God, why hast Thou forsaken me?' "

In 1958 a place was found for *Peace,* a place where planes were zooming overhead, where cars rushed to and fro, where people had no time to look up and think of, much less admire, *Peace.* The San Francisco International Airport would be her new home, and Benny, almost a beggar, could not be a chooser. "Miss Peace," as Bufano called her, was not a fashionable lady. But what nun is fashionable? *Peace* looked like a nun under a silver-leaf coif, her face in quiet repose.

"Maybe if the world gets frightened enough we'll have peace." Benny Bufano, the five foot dynamo, sighed a deep-down sigh. Then he said, as an afterthought: "Man is a stupid beast. He seldom learns unless he is shocked into thinking. The greatest good to thinking has been the invention of atomic fission. It is terrible in its worst aspects, but God has seen fit for it to happen so that mankind can be saved. The great force of atomic fission has blown man out of his convenient nationalism into international thinking. If it is fear that must awaken man to brotherhood and humanity . . . then let's scare the hell out of him!

"When I said this in 1950 they called me a Communist. Hell, I'm not a Communist or any other kind of 'ist.' I just like to think about things."

Benny wanted a bunch of kids at the unveiling ceremony to say "peace" in every language. As it was reported in the *San*

Francisco News of April 18, 1958:

> The Chronicle offered to bail the statue out of hock. It arranged
> for a civic ceremony which, it hoped, no official interested in peace
> would miss. Among those invited: Secretary of State Dulles, Gov-
> ernor Knight, Mayor Christopher. But it turned out, the governor
> would not show for the unveiling at the airport tomorrow if the
> mayor did. The mayor, who is running against the governor for
> senator, would not show if the governor did. Dulles, who is run-
> ning the State Department, declined his invitation and announced
> he was taking a weekend vacation instead.
>
> And finally, the Chronicle would not show, according to Benny,
> if his unfashionable friends took part in the unveiling.
>
> Benny, usually a quiet man, raised his voice in anger: "WHAT'S
> WRONG WITH PEACE!" he shouted, causing the Union League
> members of the Press and Union League Club, where he lives, to
> shift uneasily in their overstuffed chairs. It has been reported [not
> in any morning newspaper] that Benny would picket the unveil-
> ing of his own statue if peace groups couldn't take part in the
> ceremony.
>
> He denied this. "I told them," he said with dignity, "that peace
> has no enemies. I wanted everybody to come."
>
> From Los Angeles, Mayor Christopher told the News the ceremony
> had been postponed "because of some complications no one has
> outlined for me."

The statue has never had an official unveiling. The children were
never there to say peace in any language.

In 1939 Bufano had been invited to occupy a room in the
Press Club free of rent. At last he had a home, and he was so
thankful he started to sculpture a cat whose name was "Tombstone," the most famous feline since Poe's "The Black Cat." Benny
had loved working on the statue, which was one of the few works
of his that would find a home without any fuss. Its future was
guaranteed: the Press Club of San Francisco had ordered it for
a specific purpose. In the Press Club magazine, Scoop, for 1939
an article by Gerry McLean, one of the fourth estate, gives the
proper setting for the adoption of Tombstone:

> It was an auspicious evening! The Press Club's dining room was
> full. So were not a few of those present. Nabobs on hand included
> Ben Hecht and Charlie MacArthur, refugees from newspaper
> chain gangs who had hit heavy sugar with the "Front Page." Helen

Hayes, who is prettier than most of her fellow Press Club members, was about to officiate as high priestess at a christening. Yup, a christening. Tombstone's!

Beniamino Bufano, having given birth to a black granite offspring destined to become Club mascot, occupied a wheel chair, smiling bravely through the pallor of his recent accouchement. In support of Benny were his obstetrician, two blond nurses and a bottle of domestic sherry. Outside on Post Street skulked a process server disguised as Boris Karloff, the Girl in the Iron Mask, and two other guys. Already Tombstone's father was in the shadow of a paternity suit.

Nobody said a word, including Tombstone, as Miss Hayes started the christening.

"It is my great and solemn privilege," began the First Lady of the Theater, "to say . . ."

Then it happened.

A booming baritone, obligatoed by the dulcet thrumming of a guitar, echoed suddenly from wall to wall:

"*In the ancient days of Egypt, people worshipped cats;*
Their sacred felines were a noble breed.
Nowadays the kitty-fanciers love many different kinds.
From Siamese to Persians, yes, indeed."

Well, sir, you could have heard a highball glass shatter in the sudden hush that followed. As a matter of fact, several did.

Miss Hayes, with characteristic aplomb, began again: "It is my great and solemn privilege . . ."

Again the baritone voice smothered hers like a circus tent:

"*There are many stupid cranks who prefer the Tailless Manx,*
But I know one cat that puts them in the shade.
Their pets to me look shabby when I think of that grand tabby,
That black bastard that our pal Bufano made."

A stern-faced few rose up, murder, mayhem and Martinis in their eyes. They had spotted the singing interloper, a stoutish character thumbing his guitar and wearing an egg-soiled sports jacket, white socks and a red neck. Miss Hayes stemmed the incipient riot with the raise of a delicate hand.

"It's Will Aubrey,"* said La Hayes gently. "Let him get that song off his larynx."

Tombstone preserved his silence.

The baritone, now identified, continued his role as troubadour.

---

*The late Will Aubrey, an old-time vaudeville singer and much-loved troubadour of the Press Club, where he resided for many years.

Tombstone remained hushed.

"I wonder what he thinks as he sits there so serene.
I wonder if he is a he, or if her thoughts are clean.
It seems to have sagacity
Without undue loquacity.
What wondrous perspicacity!
That cat of ebon shade.
Does he think of other pussies? Does he dream of nights gone by?
Does he think of long-gone conquests 'neath a starlit midnight sky?
That sly and so imperious
Jet animal so mysterious —
That suave but never serious
Black cat Bufano made!"

Benny Bufano, the Press Club darling, sat in the wheel chair, tears of happiness in his eyes.

Tombstone became the mascot of the San Francisco Press Club. With a knowing, self-confident look on its dark face, yet never disclosing even a hint of what it knew, the statue soon became a symbol of the Press Club's most important tradition. With Tombstone on the table, the speaker of the evening would know that all remarks were privileged and would never appear as copy. The number of V.I.P.'s that the black kitten's silence has reassured includes: Vice-President Henry Wallace; Jack Benny; Governor — later Chief Justice — Earl Warren; Henry Kaiser; Lt. Col. Gregory ("Pappy") Boyington, U.S.M.C.; Mackenzie King; Sir Thomas Beecham; Lord Halifax; Trygve Lie; J. Christiaan Smuts; and many others. At last, one of Benny's sculptures had received the affection and appreciation that it deserved.

12 ، The Political Activist

In the summer of 1939 a group of Benny's animals was to be placed in the Aquatic Park Casino on San Francisco Bay. Benny did not know much about Aquatic Park, except that it had been built by W.P.A. workers and that it was meant for the people to use. When he went to the casino to study where his animals were to be located, he discovered that the building had been leased by the city to a private concessionaire and was being operated as a night club. Indignantly he refused to allow his art to be placed in the casino. "I would rather have kids playing over my statues," he exploded, "than to have drunks stumbling over them. And I'm no teetotaler either."

Benny noticed that on the wall behind the soda fountain there was a price list printed in large black letters: COFFEE — 10 cents, COCA COLA — 10 cents, TEA — 15 cents, ORANGE JUICE — 15 cents. . . . But he didn't bother to wait and read the rest. Fifteen cents for an eyedropper full of orange juice! This shocked Benny. He looked around some more: there were no tables for people who didn't buy their food at the fountain, and kids couldn't dress or take showers for free, as the W.P.A. had planned. The concessionaires had taken over, had robbed the people of what was rightfully theirs. Public property had become private property. Bufano seethed. No trespassing! No loitering! No anything — unless you had the money to pay. This was not the way Benny interpreted the spirit of the W.P.A. He went to see people, important people; he wrote letters, but there were few answers.

"Crooks and finaglers are taking happiness and even money away from the people," he yelled at some of the city politicians.

Then things began to happen: Danysh was dismissed from the W.P.A. and Joseph Allen took his place. Bufano had not only lost a friend, but he felt miserable; still he kept on fighting. With no assistance from the local San Francisco office, he took off for Washington, but not before the *San Francisco News* sent reporters out to see for themselves what was happening at Aquatic Park. They found prices high, rooms closed and verandas cluttered. The famous Rainbow Room had a heavy rope knotted across the entrance. The temperature was over 90 degrees on that September day, but there was no place open for soda pop. No one was to be seen on the sun deck. The view from the radio tower was excellent, but no one came up from the crowded beach to enjoy it.

Bufano took a train to Washington, where he related his story to many of the top men on the W.P.A. They told him they knew, from their previous visits to San Francisco, that "these rats" he was talking about had foolproof protection from politicians and crooks, but Benny spoke too frankly: those robbers would kill him if he didn't watch out. They offered to get him a job in Washington, temporarily, while they conducted an investigation. It would be the safest thing for him.

"To hell with being safe," was Benny's reply. "My life, anybody's life, isn't worth a damn if we have to be afraid to speak the truth. I may be crazy, but I'm going out there right now and let them have more of it." They sent three investigators along to protect Bufano.

Benny loved the W.P.A. He loved it despite the agony and misery he suffered. He loved it because he could produce. He loved it because it was the one way he knew that his country could achieve his great ideal — that of making America not the mechanical, materialistic society it had become but the America of culture, wisdom and kindliness.

In a speech Bufano expressed these thoughts:

Once they make up their minds, the American people can do anything. Their desire for full living and their eagerness in acquiring an education about the arts, the sciences, and most important, human relations . . . all add up to an exciting fact. It is a demonstration that we might well guide the future course of world destiny to a better life.

The vastness of our country inclines our engineers to think in broad terms. Witness our dams and our bridges. They point the way to our new American culture. Their very designs reflect public service and functional objectives. That is why they are remarkably beautiful. And that is why our great American public make pilgrimages to these public monuments as Europeans do to shrines.

Industry, too, has inadvertently contributed to the raising of our aesthetic standards. Our airplanes, our automobiles, our streamlined trains . . . all embody in their designs that economy of line that is true art. But herein lies a great paradox!

Too many of the same people who relish the modern, streamlined simplicity of our cars and trains object to a sculptor using simple lines and pure forms in trying to put across his message. Yet, this same group readily accepts the sculptural forms of ancient Egypt because they have been told authoritatively that these forms are good. Are they good because they are ancient and Egyptian, or are they good because they are good?

Apparently, there has been a lack of education on aesthetic appreciation. Johnny and Mary have been taught typing and how to punch a cash register, but they have not, as yet, received the fuller measure of knowledge found in less transient values but bequeathing more permanent happiness. This is also the job of the artist, who must not only be satisfied in creating a work of art but should also be a public relations man and an educator as well.

Benny returned to San Francisco and the investigation began. For days investigators interviewed people and checked records. Benny continued working in his W.P.A. studio, waiting for an official assignment to begin work on the fantastic frieze, 183 feet long and 12 feet high, for the George Washington High School. Then, in an editorial of the *San Francisco News*, dated November 25, 1939, a headline blazed forth with:

AQUATIC PARK VICTORY!

The battle of Aquatic Park has been won on behalf of the people. . . . Henceforth the million-dollar project will be a public recreation place in fact as well as in name.

So ends in victory a fight taken up at first by Beniamino Bufano, sculptor, who did some of the decorations and felt the people were not getting a chance to enjoy them.

Benny, triumphant, started to work on the George Washington High School frieze, approved by both the W.P.A. and the Board of Education. Trouble started immediately. Benny didn't like Allen, who had taken Danysh's place, and he equally disliked Dorothy Collins, Allen's secretary. They, in turn, felt Benny was a snooper and a troublemaker; they did everything to make him uncomfortable, Benny said later. He was supposed to be in complete control of the frieze project but was never consulted on any changes. They gave him no studio to work in. He was also accused of carving the features of Harry Bridges, the labor leader, and of Russia's Lenin into the frieze.

"They're crazy! Bridges and Lenin are nowhere to be found in my works," Benny insisted. "Of course I didn't drag my faces for the project out of thin air. There are likenesses of Washington, Lincoln, Jefferson, city officials and W.P.A. officials — all, you see, good clean American stuff. I even have the symbol of the two Roosevelts: FDR on Teddy's horse. Certainly, nothing could be more American than Teddy's horse."

On Friday, March 15, 1940, a padlock was put on Benny's door and he was handed his 403, the severance notice from the project.

"My original drawing and design had been removed from the studio, and although my letter of dismissal said that I was entitled to my tools and art works, there was nothing in there that I could take."

Benny's friends and fellow sculptors on the project wrote a presentation, asking for Benny's reinstatement: "We believe that the inefficient progress of work was and is attributable to lack of cooperation due to personal antagonism to Beniamino Bufano upon the part of the Federal Art Project Administration." Many prominent people, the Board of Education and the entire press backed Bufano and insisted that he be reinstated. One report from Washington declared that the mess reflected "primarily against Allen and not Bufano."

The *San Francisco Call* wondered "what Joseph Allen, who fired Bufano from the art project, is going to do now . . . now that the Board of Education had so definitely announced that it wants Bufano back on the huge bas-relief he was doing . . . for George Washington High School."

Because things were going so slowly, Benny wanted to go to Washington. Two of Benny's best friends, Leon Liebes and John D. Short, sent him a joint letter telling him they did not think it desirable for him to make the trip:

> Washington is nearing the election campaign period, and they certainly have no desire to alienate any of their officials. . . . You must understand, Benny, that you and Washington have two very different views. You appear to think that Washington is ready, eager, and willing to fight for ideals and the conception of justice, as might appear to each individual. This is very far from the true state of affairs. Washington . . . does not want to champion the cause of the individual.

Benny went to Washington anyway but got nowhere.

Because Bufano had so much difficulty getting back on the W.P.A., he was hired by Aubrey Williams, national head of the National Youth Administration, to become director of the art project for the N.Y.A. in San Francisco. Benny started to work; he borrowed a record player and some Bach records from a pianist friend, and with the music as his inspiration he worked night and day at a statue of Bach.

In 1935 he had done several studies of Bach, with the idea in mind of creating a sculpture for the Bach Festival in Carmel, California. In November, 1937, he wrote to a friend: "I was really very serious last night when we spoke of doing a study of Bach in Carmel. I have had this in mind for nearly two years and have made a number of studies on it." In February, 1938, he sent the same letter to seven people in Carmel Highlands, stating that he needed about $700 for granite and stainless steel, and asking that each contribute $100. But, as Benny frequently had difficulties getting the money, it was not until 1942 that he was able to complete the work, apparently without cooperation from the citizens of Carmel. He completed the Bach statue while still on N.Y.A., and Carmel officials, hearing of it, asked Bufano if they could borrow it for the week-long festival. He agreed. The statue was shipped to Carmel and the artist followed. However, things rarely went smoothly for Benny and this was no exception.

13 ' Little Lady of the Stones

High on a scaffold, Bufano was putting the finishing touches to the Bach statue in readiness for the unveiling the following day. A slender girl stood watching him. Her dress was a dark gray, like the quiet dress of a nun, and her eyes were lifted to the statue as though she were praying. Bufano smiled down at her, then went on with his work. An hour passed and at last he descended the scaffold.

She was sitting on a near-by bench, waiting. "It is a beautiful statue, Mr. Bufano," she said. . . . "Do you ever take pupils?"

Bufano examined the sensitive face and knew that "here was no predatory female flattering me for some deep and underhanded reason." He said: "I'd like to teach you. What's your name?"

"Muriel," she said. "May I come for a lesson sometime?"

"Right now."

She didn't seem surprised at his abruptness and her eyes brightened. They walked to the studio that had been set up for him in Carmel. Bufano got together a lunch of fruit and cheese and milk; she helped him as though they had been friends for many years. They talked as they prepared the simple meal and ate it.

"How long will you be in Carmel after the festival?" she asked.

"I gotta get back to San Francisco right after. I've got lots of work to do."

"Oh." She looked a bit disappointed. "What's the good of my starting lessons if you're going off to San Francisco?"

"What's stopping you from coming up with me?"

She shrugged her shoulders, a little embarrassed. "It doesn't cost much to live here, in Carmel."

"If you need a place to sleep, you can always use my studio," he offered.

"Thanks a lot . . . but maybe I can make other arrangements."

"Is your family in San Francisco?"

"No, they're all in New York."

"How come you decided to be a sculptor?"

"I always loved to make mud pies," she laughed. "Isn't that the stock answer? Seriously though, I've always loved the feel and color of stones. I like to work in stone. It's sort of a passion with me."

"You're such a delicate-looking girl, it's strange that you like to work in stone." To Benny this quiet, gentle girl sitting before him was a new experience.

Several hours later, when the art lesson was finished, Bufano self-consciously asked, "May I walk you home, Muriel?"

"Of course, Beniamino."

They walked along the white sand of the Carmel ocean front, and as they walked she picked up small stones whose shell-like pinks and pearly grays delighted her. Their smooth, sea-washed surfaces were pleasing to the touch of her slender fingers. As she gathered the stones she showed them to Benny. He took each one and talked of its beauty. Then she put them into the pocket of her full skirt.

"I've got a new name for you, Muriel."

"You have?"

"The Little Lady of the Stones," he answered. "You're like a little saint."

"You're deeply religious, aren't you? You're very much like a priest . . . a very wonderful priest that I know."

"I don't go in for formal religion or going to church, but I believe God is everywhere."

"I find my religion in the church," she said as she stopped at the gate of her small bungalow.

"I'll call for you in the morning for the unveiling," he said.

Early the next morning, Bufano came to escort Muriel to the festival. The warm July sun greeted them; the picturesque streets of Carmel were filled with a happy carnival spirit. Suddenly, as they neared the plaza, his heart sank. He noticed a change in the gathering crowd. Benny heard loud, angry and indignant voices. The statue wasn't standing there. Muriel looked up and cried, "Oh! How terrible!"

Bufano was paralyzed. His statue lay on the ground, its blue stone head had been wrenched from the stainless-steel body and stolen.

There had been much criticism of the statue, but critics joined with admirers in condemning the destruction and theft. Conjecture had it that the vandals may have been "super patriots" objecting to Bach's nationality; others felt that the wreckers might be antagonists of Bufano himself, perhaps from San Francisco.

Margaret Valiant, national director of the N.Y.A., said: "Anonymous destruction is one thing that completely floors me. I have the greatest respect for the person who will come out in open controversy. We disagree violently but we disagree openly. I don't care what a man believes, if he comes out and says what he believes, I respect him. But this vandalism in the dark . . . !"

Since the statue was Federal property having been made by artists on the National Youth Administration working with Bufano, the vandalism was reported to the F.B.I. Benny was interviewed by an F.B.I. agent: "Who do you think did this, Mr. Bufano?"

"I can't imagine," Benny replied. "Must have been done by somebody who understands sculpture, though. The head was attached to an armature. That's an iron pole rising inside the body. It would take considerable knowledge to remove the head from the body."

"Have you got any enemies?"

"Sure! I've plenty of friends and enemies."

Bufano returned from Carmel to find his garage studio at 1940 Laguna Street a shambles! Bufano stood speechless. "My priceless Chinese art objects were torn and broken on the floor. My sketches trodden by muddy feet and water soaked. My four portfolios of drawings were gone. My work bench and table were overturned and my tools damaged. Even walnuts, my only food supply, were smashed underfoot on the floor. Upstairs in my bedroom, my personal letters and papers had been ransacked, my few clothes were torn and dirtied." Benny, gazing forlornly at the devastation, called the police. The four portfolios were later found in the car of a minister and returned to the artist.

"I don't mind someone stealing," he said, "but to destroy . . . that is a crime against the world! They destroyed my Bach statue, and now this. It was more than I could bear. I just broke down and cried like a baby.

"I remember when I was about thirteen. In those days you had to put a quarter in the meter to get gas for light and cooking. I wanted to paint, but it was nighttime. My father was not home. I begged my mother to turn on the gas so I could see to paint. My mother always used to give me my way, so she slipped me a quarter to put in the meter. I went into the back room to make some sketches of my mother and Remo. Remo and I were always pretty close. So while I was sketching in the flickering gas light, the door was suddenly pushed open and there was my father. You could smell that he had been drinking some Dago red wine, maybe with some beer thrown in.

"'You bum,' said my father, lunging at me. 'Here I lose my job and you spend all my money burning up the gas. Where the hell do you think the money comes from?' Funny thing, my father calling me a bum with him doing the drinking. Anyway, I was in for it. He took a razor strop he had brought with him and lashed me across the back. Being a little guy I could hop back and forth across the room without getting hit much. Several times, when he missed me, he fell flat on the floor. This irritated him so much that he looked around the room for something else to hit me with. Then I could tell by the look in his eyes that he had found the best weapon. It was my drawings.

"He picked up one of them and said, 'Maybe you'll remember this for the rest of your life.' He held the drawing sidewise, then placed it over the gas flame till it caught fire. I stood against the wall, dumbfounded. Then he burned all my other sketches and paintings. My throat was so jammed with emotion and hatred that I almost choked. 'Never let me catch you wastin' your time on art crap again, you understand?' And with that my father stumbled out the door.

"I can still feel myself picking up the pieces of ash that had been my work and it all crumbled in my fingers. My tears dropped onto my hands as I felt about in the dark for some salvaged drawings. That was the first time my work had been destroyed, but I was to learn that it wouldn't be the last, or the worst.

"If he wanted to, all he had to do was reach over and beat me to a pulp. I was so shocked that I was paralyzed. He came back into the room again, told me to get to hell to bed, and then turned out the gas."

For many months Muriel came daily to study with Benny in his studio. They always played records while they worked; Bach, Mozart and Beethoven were their favorites. She was as poor as he: they shared their meals and talked of their work, of art, books, music and philosophy. Each day he eagerly awaited her coming, always a little worried that she wouldn't appear. She seemed to him to be a lovely, heavenly creature who would one day disappear and never return. He fell deeply in love with her.

One day she suddenly rested her head in her arms and started crying. Beniamino put his arm around her. "What's happened, Muriel?"

She told him that her folks couldn't afford to take care of her. They wanted her to come home. She didn't want to go home; she had never been as happy as she was working with him. She felt her only way out was to become a nun — she had been thinking of it for a long time.

"A nun!" exclaimed Benny. "You can't become a nun! You're a fine artist! I'll take care of you! I'll share everything I have with you!"

Muriel put her hand on his lovingly. "I know you will, Beniamino."

"Then why go away? I need you, Muriel. Your friendship is the dearest thing I have in life."

She waited a moment, as though she expected him to continue. He was silent. "I must do what my faith demands, Beniamino." She clasped his hand lovingly and left.

Although she returned daily for her lessons in the weeks that followed, Benny sensed that he was losing her. Tormented, he did not know what to do. In desperation he talked to friends and wrote letters to them, seeking help. But Benny's last hope failed: there was no response, and finally the day came when Muriel entered a convent.

That night Benny lay on his bed, his eyes stark. His deep sorrow had become religious ecstasy. She had become the bride of Christ; she was cloistered and forever lost to him. But are there not many Christs in this sad world? Is not every man whose soul has been humiliated Christ? Was not Christ the very symbol of man's inhumanity to man? And had not he, Beniamino Bufano, been made a buffoon, been laughed at and ridiculed for his work, his ideas? Yes, she was the bride of Christ and, to the extent of his own messianic feelings, she was also his, Bufano's, bride: the nun, the untouchable, the unattainable, was now his forever. Benny's spirit lifted, he fell into deep peaceful slumber.

Months later, in a letter to a friend, Benny spoke of Muriel:

This beautiful person is the most cultured person I have, in all my travels, touched hands and exchanged conversations with. A real scholar and student and the most beautiful philosopher I have ever met. I have met many men and women of philosophical and spiritual learning and understanding but never one so simple, so cultured, and so young and with such depth of spirit as this simple beautiful saint, a very shy and unassuming beautiful youth. Very quiet in her speech but with a key of understanding and knowledge as though she had been living from the beginning of time. Music, art, philosophy all wrapped in one little shy world of knowing. The most dominant element of this beautiful little saint is that she is, in her living, the symbol of her philosophy, knowledge and the living of that knowledge. I have learned more from this simple living saint than all the books, schools and philosophers in this so confused human mud-puddle, and camouflaged, greedy, human misdirected and miscarriaged society. If God is like this little saint, I am very religious. If God is the image of this greedy society, let's abandon Him. This is my religion.

I always wash my hands before I write to her at the monastery. I have been around the world twice and lived with various peoples for many years, learned part of their language and their hopes and beliefs, and shared both their joys and sorrows. All of this taught me much. Yet, somehow, it is the light that two women, my mother and this little Nun, held before me that has had the greatest influence on my life and made me most aware of God's power, His mercy and His justice. This, I believe!

Benny also wrote a poem to Muriel:

Out of the breath of space
You appeared from the faint forms of destiny.
Chanting a song real but the brief moment of a shooting star.
And now you are gone and I loved you.

Muriel was gone. Bufano couldn't work: his hammers and chisels became unwieldy, his hands clumsy, his eyes always on the door expectantly. Finally he cast aside his tools and ran out to wander the streets. Hours later he found himself more than a hundred miles away from San Francisco, in the isolated refuge of his studio at Big Sur.

"I have no recollection of how I got there. I had never been one to talk to anyone about my sorrows or my problems. But this time I needed someone to talk to. I started up the road leading to the home of Henry Miller, the writer, who was my close friend. As I was walking up the hill the Little Sister of the Stones appeared beside me. I put my hand out and grasped her around the waist so that she wouldn't fall over the cliff. But she wasn't there. And I became frightened. And afraid. Afraid of what was happening to me."

When he finally reached Miller's place he was so sick and feverish that Miller's wife, Lepska, tried to put him to bed. He fought against it but finally, near midnight, went to bed. About three o'clock in the morning he got up; he felt as if he were in another world, as though what was going on came from another body. Slipping into his shoes, he ran down the hill and across the highway toward his studio. Later, he remembered Miller trying to catch up with him and convince him to take it easy. "From what Henry told me, I sure must have been crazy."

Bufano remembered the brightness of the early morning glare coming through the heavy fog banks the next morning. He swore

that he saw the Little Sister of the Stones retracing her steps up
the hill, finally lifting herself off the ground and disappearing
with the swirling fog. The poet in him once more burst forth
as he stood watching the windblown fog-clouds follow his love.

> The sun, as usual peeped his golden face
> And smiled awhile to the soul
> When suddenly the clouds were hurried by the winds
> Chasing the earth in the deep dark abysmal night

The next day Bufano went back to work on an enormous redwood burl which he had been carving into an owl on previous
visits to Big Sur.

Soon Benny found separation from Muriel unbearable and
one day he hitched a ride to the convent in the Santa Cruz
Mountains, where the church had sent Muriel for her probation-
ary period. He spoke to the mother superior, offering a gift to
the convent — a mural on one of the walls. The mother superior,
assuming that a man with a name like Bufano would be a good
Catholic, accepted his offer gladly. Benny acquired a studio outside the walls of the convent.

In the days that followed, Benny complained that he needed
some assistance. He wondered if, by chance, there happened to
be anyone in the convent who was an artist. The mother superior, with a twinkle in her eyes, said, "I'll be delighted to help
you, Mr. Bufano! Painting is my hobby!" However, after working a few days she said, "I'm really quite busy, Mr. Bufano, but
I have an able substitute. She tells me she was a student of a
very fine sculptor." The next day Muriel and a companion nun
became Bufano's assistants.

Although Muriel was always with another nun, Bufano managed to slip her a note in a pad of gold leaf, which was used
extensively in the background of the mural. He suggested a
hiding place at the north end of the garden where they could
exchange letters. At first her letters were warm and full of
reminiscences of their former companionship. Then the letters
became impersonal and formal, finally ceasing entirely. Benny,
realizing that Muriel had become completely absorbed in the
monastic life, hurriedly completed the mural. Before leaving for

San Francisco he spoke to the mother superior: "This has been a deep religious experience for me, and my association with my little assistant has been like being with a saint."

Back in San Francisco, the full impact and tragedy of the vandalism he had suffered hit him hard. In protest Bufano made a ten-foot fresco of a cowled St. Francis, eyes staring from the head, mouth open in a mad scream of denunciation. He called it *Anathema Against San Francisco*.

"This vandalism was the last straw," Bufano told reporters. "I didn't mind the criticisms, the rebuffs in San Francisco all these years. I figured some day people would understand. But this . . . this was different. I only wanted to beautify San Francisco. I figure it's time for me to give up and leave."

When Bufano's statement came out in the press, a group of men anxious to keep Benny in San Francisco, headed by attorneys Jake Ehrlich and Sol Silverman, decided to incorporate Bufano.* A sum of money would be collected and put into a fund, giving him a monthly income and a place to work that would be protected from vandalism. This, like so many other plans and schemes to help the artist, soon folded.

Later, in 1946, Benny began an investigation as to the whereabouts of all the sculptures he had made in the days of the W.P.A. and which belonged to the City of San Francisco. He found them stored — or rather, dumped — in the city yard behind the Laguna Honda Hospital. It was a disillusioned, almost tearful Bufano who viewed the debris, for his precious life's works were lying there broken and defaced. Nine of his pieces were smashed, decapitated or mutilated.

In October of 1946 Newspaperman's Post No. 116, the Fred Bunch Post of the American Legion, joined in the fight to preserve from vandals the priceless sculptures of Comrade Beniamino Bufano. A mass meeting of the post was called and pictures of the destruction were shown. The large group went to the super-

---

*Bufano, Inc., was a forerunner of the Bufano Society of the Arts, an influential group of friends who helped manage his finances. The Society was named in Bufano's will as executor of his estate and legal owner of his works.

visors' chambers in City Hall to present the resolution and to voice its protests. The resolution called the supervisors' attention to the vicious wrecking of the Bufano works stored in the yard; asked that what remained of Bufano's work be found and its condition ascertained; that the board set about at once to safeguard these works; that responsibility for the failure to safeguard them be fixed; that salvageable art be protected; and that Bufano be asked to restore or direct the restoration of damaged pieces to their original condition.

Bufano's own theory about the works of a sculptor was that they remain the property of the artist during his lifetime. Any commissions he may have received for his creations are merely contributions to the furtherance of art! As any prudent man does, Benny kept a protective eye on his property. And this leads to the penguin at Aquatic Park.

During the war, the Aquatic Park facilities had been used by the military as a vehicle headquarters. It was inevitable that a certain amount of damage would be done, and done it was. When the Federal government released the property to the city, apparently an offer was made to pay for the damage and have the structure restored to its former beauty, but despite a lot of talk and criticism nothing was done by the San Francisco Park Commission. A once picturesque monument remained neglected, crumbling, unkempt, dirty — a blot on the landscape. Just at the entrance to the park stood Bufano's three-ton penguin. Once a gleaming, stainless-steel and polished red porphyry work of art, it was now wrecked by vandals, with its stainless-steel head stolen, its stonework defaced and broken. The Park Commission and its superintendent turned a deaf ear to Benny's years of pleading that the statue be repaired.

In 1949 Bufano took his case to the construction industry, where he found people motivated by strong civic pride. In the dead of the night, these men earned distinction as patrons of the arts by carting the penguin away, thus rescuing it from the low estate into which it had fallen. Park Superintendent Girod was furious. He had the law on his side and public property *had* been stolen, but he stirred up a hornet's nest when San

Francisco was reminded that nothing had been done to restore Aquatic Park! The superintendent cooled down when money, materials, labor and work space were provided by individuals so that Bufano could restore his creation to its former glory. There was nothing for the Park Commission to do but give its sanction.

Bufano restored this beautiful sculpture, sometimes called *The Prayer* since the head of the huge penguin lifts itself to Heaven as though in prayer. The wings gently and lovingly enfold two baby penguins at its feet. This magnificent work of art was placed at the entrance to Rickey's Restaurant, although its beautiful granite base was still broken.

In 1953 Benny asked that the city return all his statues because he, and not the city, really owned them! A survey was ordered of Benny's works; a search of old Art Commission minutes from ten years back disclosed that the city owned two heads, two fish and a group of three children, also a mask of St. Francis in copper, a *Mother of Races* and a *Peace* in grey granite. All seemed to be either lost, strayed or stolen, and nowhere to be found. Bufano claimed that the *Peace*, the torso and a pair of unidentified arms, two fish and the group of children belonged to him.

In 1956 restless Benny went bear hunting. He was trying to locate not only his sculpture of a bear, which had disappeared many years before, but also twelve pieces of valuable granite bought by the Federal government for sculptors during the days of the W.P.A. The bear was found at the Southeast Sewage Treatment Plant, at Phelps Street and Jerrold Avenue, quietly hibernating on a piece of granite atop a sand dune. Art Commissioner Bernard C. Beglay, who helped Bufano find the bear and the twelve pieces of granite, told Benny he could have the bear; Sherman P. Duckel, public works director, said the Art Commission could have the granite but couldn't give it to anyone. However, he added, "All I'm interested in is getting those twelve pieces of granite out of the way. We want to use the space."

Benny had had good reason to level anathema against San Francisco, or at least against some of its people, and most of it cannot be blamed on adolescent vandalism. Art seems to have a peculiar affinity for the lunatic fringe of people who wish to destroy. Of course, even artists themselves destroy their own works, but this is called perversity rather than vandalism. No matter what happened to him, however, Benny was inclined to be philosophical about his life. Not that he didn't struggle to improve his own as well as the world's lot, but he seemed to be able to take the good with the bad.

There is no more vicious indicator of what has happened to some of Bufano's works than the story told by the plate index of *Bufano,* an outsized book of some of Benny's beautiful works published in Florence in 1956. His woes are succinctly pictured: *David,* destroyed in 1916; *St. Francis of Assisi,* destroyed 1927; Head, stolen . . . whereabouts unknown . . . destroyed by fire . . . never returned . . . and on and on.

In his lifetime, Bufano had come to expect vandalism, yet he did nothing to prevent temptation. He seldom locked his studio doors, either through forgetfulness or disdain. His door was always open in the deserted schoolroom he used as a studio off the main highway in Big Sur. Even the most casual of friends were invited to visit him there. It was not too difficult to find; wandering campers and strolling bums often stumbled across the place. Once inside, a person was confronted with statuary, paintings and tapestries from China. "Thousands of dollars worth of stuff around here," Benny would say proudly to his friends. Then he would point to a sign over the door which read:

Come in, Look Around
Close the Door After You
Please Leave Things As They Are
I Trust You
Have a Good Time

For years, Bufano used to remark that people were basically honest, and that they wouldn't take anything if you appealed to their sense of honesty and fair play. Yet, one day when he returned to his studio at Big Sur and found everything stolen, he shrugged his shoulders, said "bastards" under his breath and then remarked, "That's people for you."

He never quite gave up on the human race. "There is salvation for everybody. Even for those bastards who have vandalized me almost out of existence. I don't know who wrecked my things, although I have my ideas, but I forgive them. They are to be pitied rather than censured. Sure, I've been mad. I had a right to be, but I've never done anything to hurt anybody. With all the vandalism against me and my works, the only hostility I took out on people was to make the ten-foot fresco of an angry St. Francis."

Bufano, disappointed at the failure of the scheme to incorporate him, went to New York to see his family in 1944. By the time he reached New York, however, his anger had subsided and he was lonely for San Francisco, his friends there and his work. After staying only a few days in New York, he arranged to return to California.

14 ʼ You CAN Fight City Hall

It was early in March, 1944, that Bufano, his briefcase tucked under his arm, stomped down the gangway of a big plane at the San Francisco Airport into the waiting arms of several of his friends, most of them from the press, who greeted him with elaborate salaams and joyful congratulations. He thought the war was over and asked if it was. They informed him that the war was just started and that Mayor Roger Lapham wanted to see him as soon as he landed.

Bufano, puzzled, wondered what he had done to cause the wrath of the mayor. "I couldn't figure it out. Maybe those crazy press boys were playing a joke on me." With a great show of solemnity they ushered the artist into a waiting car, and he was whisked away to the mayor's office.

There Bufano shook hands with the genial, plump, white-haired, beaming Mayor Lapham. His Honor wasted no words but asked Bufano how he would like to be the new art commissioner. Bufano thought it was all a big joke, but the mayor, seeing that Bufano didn't believe him, convinced him that he was the man to fill a vacancy on the Art Commission, explaining that it needed some new blood. Benny was elated but told the mayor that the members of the commission wouldn't like what he had to tell them. Apparently this was exactly what the mayor wanted. He said he knew Bufano to be a man with ideas — and good ones, at that. The Art Commission hadn't had the semblance of a new idea for years, and that he was sure Bufano would liven things up considerably, judging from his former actions on the W.P.A.

Bufano accepted and said he wanted to get on the job at once. The mayor agreed that they had better act fast; if he didn't get Benny sworn in immediately, the vultures would be coming in so fast and furious for his head that neither of them would be in public life long. The mayor summoned the registrar and two witnesses, and swore Bufano in as art commissioner.

As Benny walked out of the mayor's office, a man came up to him with his hand outstretched. Thinking the man was congratulating him upon his new appointment, Benny put out his hand. When he drew it back he had a summons in it.

"Of all the dirty, stinkin' tricks," exploded Bufano. He had no idea what he was being summoned for. Opening it, he found that his wife, Virginia Howard Bufano, whom he had married in 1925 and left three months later, was suing him for nonsupport of his putative child. Apparently Virginia had had enough of Benny's dalliance. She felt that she had been unable to get her share of his works, according to the agreement of 1931, and since then Benny had been continually written up as receiving important commissions, which to her nose meant cash. Now she wanted either his art works or his money. "She knows damned well I don't have any money," said Benny, "and she can't get my art works because they don't belong to me. I own nothing to give away." Benny started to tear up the summons, but his friends told him it wouldn't do for a new commissioner to flout the law.

Bufano went to San Rafael, across the Bay north of San Francisco, where his case was tried the following week. Denying that the child was his, he testified that he had lived with his wife only three months and that he had had no relations with her after that. He told the court that he was an art commissioner of San Francisco and the judge would have a lot of explaining to do if he were jailed. Benny, never one to respect the law or its minions, had done it again. The judge could have dismissed the case, or given Bufano up to ten days.

"Ten days in jail," said the judge. "Take him away." And the artist was led away to the Marin County Jail. Swarms of reporters dropped in upon the picturesque town of San Rafael and prominent people in all walks of life visited Bufano. After that, the Marin County Jail was not quite the same.

Benny found that the jail could stand many reforms. For one thing, the officials were not education-minded. Benny read aloud to the inmates a recently published book entitled *The Dove Brings Peace*. When the guards asked him to stop because he was disturbing the calm of the jail, Bufano replied, "I'm just making the prisoners' lives more worthwhile," and continued to read.

"Talk about persecution," said Benny, "this jail is worse than the Death March. There's no room for exercise or recreation. When I get out of here I'm going to design a modern jail. And the ventilation here is terrible too. During the day it isn't so bad, but at night when they close the windows and lock you in . . . it stinks!"

One newspaperman, a stranger to Bufano, asked if he'd like to have a cigarette. "Never smoke," said the prisoner, "but I would like some oranges." Then he thought for a moment. "No, I don't want oranges just for myself. These other guys here need them more than I do." The next day crates of oranges were delivered to the jail, and Benny was happy. The halls and corridors of the Marin County Jail were cluttered with boxes of fruit. The janitor was wild, the judge perplexed.

Bananas, oranges, all kinds of fruit! People kept Bufano and the jail supplied with food of many kinds, but mainly food for a vegetarian. The prisoners had never had it so good, and probably neither have prisoners in any other jail. On the third day, however, everything stopped: no more fruit, no more outside food. The jail had become a veritable market and dealers were complaining. Back to the same old meals went the prisoners, moaning and groaning, muttering, ". . . and they've got saltpeter in the food."

"That settles it for me," said Bufano, and he began a fast. No food did he eat that day, nor the next. Other prisoners joined him, and on the fifth day no one ate any food. From the first Bufano had asked for a sheet and a pillow but none had been forthcoming. On this fifth day he got the sheet and pillow, but he refused to take it unless the other prisoners could have the same. There were not enough to go around so Benny went without.

On the sixth day Bufano was called into the judge's chambers. The judge told him that he had decided to cut his sentence to six days. He was a free man.

"I am not," said Bufano. "You gave me a ten-day sentence and ten days it'll be." He went back into his cell amid the cheers of the other prisoners, who had learned through the grapevine that Bufano was to be set free.

Later that day a newspaperman told him, "Don't be crazy. Get out when you can. San Francisco needs you more on the Art Commission than San Rafael needs you in jail." Bufano quit jail on the sixth day, much to the relief of all those connected with law enforcement. The prisoners, however, were glum: no jail had ever been like this.

When Bufano arrived back in San Francisco, he was a greater hero to the press and the people than ever before, and a greater thorn in the side of the deadheads, dead beats, and dead ducks. After his six days in jail, Benny felt that probably nothing worse could happen to him. "That was a terrible experience," he moaned to one of his friends. "Hardened criminals are put in the same room with poor innocent guys," and after a slight hesitation he added, "like me." Then he laughed. "Well, I'm glad to be back so I can get started on the Art Commission. I've got my life mapped out for me if I'm to put new blood into those deadheads, as the mayor wants me to."

Bufano started off simply enough with the Art Commission. He went to the office for the Art Commission meetings. It was locked. He found no one with any keys. He asked when the Art Commission met. No one knew. Who sent out notices? What notices? Benny went to Mayor Lapham and asked if there was an Art Commission or not — he couldn't find it.

Lapham told him not to be so impatient. There *was* a so-called Art Commission, but it wouldn't meet till next week, or maybe it was the week after. He wasn't sure when, being too busy to keep up with the inactivities of the Art Commission.

"It seemed everybody else was too busy," Bufano said. "Nobody on the commission even wanted to talk to me. When I told the mayor this, he reminded me of the Aquatic Park incident and maybe they were afraid to talk to me. They knew I was a fighter.

"Hell, I'm not a fighter. I just try to look for the truth, that's all. The mayor's answer to this was that truth always was a dangerous business. And the truth-seeker was always a hated man. . . ."

Benny soon put life into the commission's meetings. Newspaper headlines gave a rundown on some of his activities:

COMPLETELY UNIMPRESSED SCULPTOR SAYS ART COMMISSION SHOULD ABOLISH ITSELF!

BATTLE FLARES ANEW AT ART BOARD MEETING.

BARROOM EPITHET CHARGED TO BUFANO: LAPHAM ATTENDS SESSION

One editorial said in part:

The effect of the Bufano membership on the board is neither imaginary nor uncertain.

For better or worse, the commission has been more in the public eye since the diminutive sculptor became a member than in all the previous years of its history.

Another editorial practically pleaded with Bufano to take it easy:

Art Commissioner Beniamino Bufano has learned, with a profound shock, we presume, that politics is an art far more esoteric than sculpture. . . . Both sculptor and politician require proficiency in chiseling, but there's a difference. Whereas the sculptor works at his chiseling, the politician chisels at his work. . . . All things considered, he should not let himself become discouraged in the City Hall maze. He should be consoled by the recollection that it took Ulysses twenty years to find his way back to Ithaca.

A few months later, Benny got into more trouble by calling members of the Art Commission "a bunch of stupid bastards." The commission members censured him in a report:

Mr. Bufano became belligerent and abusive. The Chairman repeatedly requested him to restrain himself. Mr. Bufano became more abusive, personal and profane. After adjournment, Mr.

Bufano spoke and acted in a manner entirely unbecoming to a member of the Art Commission.

"That's not true," recalled Benny, "I called myself a stupid bastard for having joined such a sterile organization as that Art Commission. I told them there wasn't one of them qualified to talk about the arts. Instead of having a musician on the commission they had the president of the A. F. of L. Musician's Local on it . . . a guy who could hardly whistle except in fear." (Benny made no bones about telling this to the man himself, who countered by telling Benny that he doubted whether the Art Commission had a sculptor.) "Furthermore, we had presidents of the Park Commission, the library, the museum, but not one good, solid librarian or park or museum worker," said Bufano.

"That first year on the Art Commission dispelled any illusions I had left after the Aquatic Park experience. Everybody thinks politics and politicians are corrupt! Well . . . it might be a good idea for every citizen to serve on an Art Commission to get the true picture. I had been warned by the mayor about what was going on in the commission but I never thought that they could be that bad. Imagine my surprise when I arrived at my first Art Commission meeting quite by accident. I was going to this room for another matter and when I got there I found myself in the middle of a meeting.

"There I was in the company of Fleishhacker, all three of him . . . with a vote in his hands for the Park Commission, another for the California Palace of the Legion of Honor, and a third as director of the de Young Museum. The way the commission was run was really laughable.

"Fleishhacker nominated a guy for the head of the Art Commission and seconded him in the next breath. Without even listening to me they made the vote unanimous. Then I began to wise up. I asked them if it wasn't possible for Fleishhacker to make a motion, then vote himself down, two-to-one, if he was not careful to do a little lobbying with himself. They never bothered to answer my question. So many members of the commission were absent it was a disgrace. One hadn't attended for a whole year. I figured anybody would and should take his job seriously, especially when working for the people. I wanted to make our city beautiful and art-conscious, but they laughed at me. It sure was discouraging."

Bufano attended his second meeting full of fire. "I can't see why a commission of ten members needs any committees," he said. "We should make it our business to know everything about all of the art forms so we can act intelligently. Committees are just a waste of time when you consider the little bit of work we do here. This commission is worse than a bunch of old women. All you do is talk. Let's have some action."

They told Bufano that they didn't have the time.

"That's a laugh," Bufano said. "They didn't have the time! Well then, everything was simple. I told them to abolish themselves. They were all a disgrace to the city. Why, if the people knew how that last meeting was held there'd have been an uproar. We rushed through the meeting as though it were nothing. The minutes showed we spent an hour and a half, but we actually spent only fifteen minutes. Why did they have to lie about such things? And who did they think they were fooling? Furthermore, the names of those who made motions were not in the record. I suggested once again, if the commissioners hadn't the time to devote to their duties here, there was only one honorable thing to do, and that's resign."

Bufano was told he was talking through his hat, and to go on with the meeting without wasting time.

"I informed them that at the last meeting they elected officers of the commission without having a quorum. That was illegal anytime and anyplace, even on the Art Commission."

The president ordered Bufano to sit down; he was correct on this point, and they would have a re-election. Bufano told them that he would sit down when he was too weak to stand. "Sitting is a sign of weakness; standing is an indication of action and strength. I don't see how we can have an election now if we don't know anything about the men eligible."

Benny was told that there were very competent men on this commission. He ignored this and read aloud a proposition asking the commission to adopt a three-point program of sponsor-

ing symphony concerts, beautifying the city by the opening of
more parks and planting more trees, and employing artists to
decorate public buildings. All of his suggestions were tabled.

The meetings rolled on, with member Bufano always in at-
tendance. He fought for his tree-planting program so vigorously
that on one occasion he was called a "runt" by one of the es-
teemed commissioners. The newspapers recorded the following:
"I don't care how much of a sculptor he is," said the music commissioner. "Nature certainly shortchanged him in a lot of other
things."

"I've been shortchanged all right," Benny said, "but not when
it comes to being honest, which is more than I can say for some
of them."

One of the San Francisco columnists on April 27, 1944, wrote:

> On the basis of demonstrated ability as a stirrer-upper, Mayor
> Lapham could do worse than make Beniamino Bufano, sculptor-
> member of the Art Commission, a roving member of all commis-
> sions. Both the Mayor and the people would learn a lot about
> what goes on in city affairs . . . some of it hush-hush indeed.

> For, while his fellow commissioners insist on treating Bufano as a
> child, Bufano had a child's ability to put his finger right on the
> spot that brings an "ouch." He's allowed to sit at the table with
> guests on the understanding of everybody except himself that he'll
> behave and keep his confounded little mouth shut.

> It's interesting to wonder whether the attitude of the commission
> would be the same if things like Bufano's question were put in
> reverse. Suppose, for instance, that Herbert Fleishhacker was pro-
> testing that Bufano shouldn't have three votes — instead of vice
> versa. Suppose Edward L. Frick was insisting that neither Bufano
> nor anybody else should be president of the commission if too busy
> with other important work to attend the meetings. It does make
> a lot of difference who asks the questions.

As he gained more experience in political circles, Bufano requested that he be given a room in City Hall. "I wanted to be
closer to the scene," he said later. "They tell me that the way to
get ahead in politics is to move right in."

He was asked to what use he would put the room?

"Creative, I replied, to creative use. And for all the people,
not just for the few who now are able to afford the money. And

I wanted to have a washroom and a telephone," Benny went on. "I might have put in a gas plate and a couch, something like the press boys have. I expected to be working at all hours trying to keep track of what became of constructive proposals for municipal betterment." Bufano didn't get his room, but he was able to arrange for the use of one, which actually gave him more than he had asked for.

At his next meeting he was pleasantly shocked to find a sub-committee voting $50,000 for the beautification of the city by recommending the planting of trees. Then, two committees also approved unanimously that the city sponsor and subsidize another one of his pet projects — having master artists touch up the city's buildings. "The function of the arts," said Benny, "is to reflect the community's spiritual expression of the people and the times through the medium of its art. It is the government's responsibility to reach this goal, uniting the people toward one common good by not only sponsoring such mediums of expression, but to encourage and foster them."

In the full meeting of the Art Commission, however, the commission referred to committee the suggestion that artists be employed to decorate public buildings. Mr. Hubbard, musician member, warned of communism creeping into the country through music and art, hinting that fifty-cent symphonies for the common people smacked of Soviet practices and were not good for America.

For the first time a member of the commission, Mr. Macky, spoke in behalf of Benny: "We have a prophet in our midst whom I feel has voiced some constructive suggestions. When we get a good shot in the arm we should seriously attempt to see what can be done about it." Then Mr. Macky turned toward Benny. "All this commission ever has done before Mr. Bufano joined us has been to pass on completed artistic matters and hire some musicians. If what Mr. Bufano says is true . . . artists should be trusted to use their own ideas in decorating buildings or we can't trust any one of our people."

"Presidents," said Bufano, "know less about what's going on in their own organizations than anybody else." He told "the old fogies" to get off the commission and let young, vigorous thinkers and doers take their places. "And there should be five members only . . . a writer, musician, sculptor, painter, and architect, instead of a sterile sixteen." Benny struggled and fought. At times it seemed everyone was against him. On other occasions, he had many backers.

An editorial in the *News* for September 19, 1944, entitled "Beniamino Appreciated," was written in reply to a reader who had asked why the newspapers had been "sardonic" in their comments about Benny's efforts to revolutionize the Art Commission:

> For *The News* we would like to enter a general demurrer to that charge. In our news and editorial columns we have tried to give favorable publicity to Mr. Bufano's aims. We believe he is sincere and right in his contention that much could be done that is not done to give more widespread enjoyment to the people in this city in all forms of artistic expression. For many years we have advocated, for instance, one of his suggestions, namely the planting of ornamental trees along the streets.
>
> If we have seemed to treat in lighter vein his maneuvers since he became a member of the Art Commission, we were only using that method to attract greater attention to his theme. It must be admitted, even by his friends, that he conducted his one-man fight in a way that made sensational news, emanating, as it did, from the hitherto hallowed confines of the Art Commission.
>
> If unorthodox methods are the best way to get results his efforts should be crowned by success, and we hope they are.

15 ⁄ The Commissioner

While Benny struggled with the other members of the Art Commission to put his ideas into practice, he also took every opportunity to express his philosophies about art and the role of the artist in a modern society.

"Artists must be employed to fill in the spaces on the walls of schools with cultural subjects in order that the students may acquire a visual education very much in the same manner that the 'old masters' were put to work on the walls of churches and public buildings. The Greeks made extensive use of their artists in sponsoring them to beautify their buildings both in and outside the walls and the adjacent grounds surrounding such buildings. The Egyptian buildings are a vast storehouse of visual education where the artists were fully sponsored by their governments, thereby fulfilling the government's artistic responsibility to the community. The records that have come down from ancient Egypt remain as vivid examples of a complete sponsorship of their contemporary art and the artist who created them.

"Let us do what we want to do. Do not censor us. Do not corrupt us. If left alone, we as artists, will do your city proud, your state, your country, your civilization. If left alone, we will find great things to do, great materials to work with, great people to immortalize. But by being left alone I don't mean you should neglect us. We need your help, and every little bit helps: your money, your encouragement, your appreciation. We even welcome your criticism, as long as your criticism is not mean, wicked or bitter.

"Then we can show you what we can do. We'll work in the most modern mediums in the world: stainless steel, duralumin and all the noncorrosive alloys. We'll work in the hardest natural mediums in the world: granite and porphyry. We'll work directly in our material, for the things we have to say are unevasive and unsentimental. Let us commemorate the great men of our time and the great cities.

"Our art must become as democratic as science and the children playing on our streets. That is why I have sculptured Pasteur, Sun Yat-sen, granite frogs, bears and seals for our parks, and St. Francis — a symbol of the city that bears his honored name, big enough to belong to everybody, too big for anyone to put in his pocket and call his own."

As usual, no one could agree about what Benny said or what he wanted to do. Occasionally a few of his ideas were permitted to ripen. For the most part, he had to call people names to stir them up. He called them names in person, over the air, in letters; he lambasted them individually and collectively.

"All people have a nostalgia for beauty," Bufano once said on a radio program. "Let us remember that the hope, the culture, the greatness, the happiness and prosperity of a great people and a great city rests not upon charity but upon justice. Today, the city hall is the most wicked habitation in the city. It is a cultural vacuum. It has its eggs all in one little basket counted by cultureless and frightened little men with dollars in their eyes . . . dollars in their ears, and dollars in their brains; and the physical feature of these men is patterned and limited to the form of the dollar sign. We must free these poor frightened little men by changing the law. I quote from Job, 'He who will lose his life by the truth shall gain both his own life and the life of the people.' Remember, you Board of Supervisors, that your job can be saved only in your fight for the good of your fellow men and humanity."

Many people did agree, however, that Benny should not waste his time on the commission. They felt that "such a talented sculptor ought to spend more time sculpting." Bufano, however, felt that sculpture had its place, but when an artist was given a chance to do some good for the great mass, he should do it and forget his own personal little interests.

He fought for an art show and got it. As the *Chronicle* said in part: "San Francisco artists were $15,000 richer. A quarter million San Franciscans, an unprecedented figure for a local art show, were richer for a closeup of the city's arts. . . . The Art Commission said that . . . the show was a huge success. Commissioner Bufano called for another show within six months. He said: 'More people came to the show in three days than come to the city's museums of art in a full year. . . . Museums are the graveyards of the artists and their directors the gravediggers!' " Altogether there were $15,000 worth of sales, and Bufano's stock went up. He was ready for his success, and those who knew Benny well could predict what might happen next. He began to drop hints here and there about music; he lectured to groups and talked over the radio about music.

"Art has the quality of unifying all men in one common language and belief," he said on one program. "Music is particularly independent of the limitations of language and free in its association and thus achieves wider acceptance among all men. Its unique rhythmic character moves large groups simultaneously and often inspires effects much more vividly than political pep talks. Music is a powerful language and a universal one, born within the hearts of every people, spoken by every human being, and cherished by every living creature on this earth. Music expresses every emotion."

Bufano was only lighting the fuse; when the explosion came no one could say that they weren't warned: he advocated a Fifty Cent Symphony. That explosion set up more explosions, but Benny never bothered to take cover; he shot his fusillades from one end of the city to the other. Then he was told that San Francisco had "one of the five best symphony orchestras in the nation. And this orchestra not only can be heard for fifty cents, but for as little as twenty-seven cents. [The concerts] are the best musical bargains in the United States. . . ."

"Bargains! That's all people think about," he said. "I didn't give a damn about cheap music. I was against segregating the poor from the rich."

Even some columnists were against Benny's concerted efforts
to have mink sit with burlap. Don Cleary in a column said:

> None can deny that when it comes to making with a chisel and
> a chunk of granite the city's Beniamino Bufano is practically in a
> class by himself. He has what the artists call intellectual integrity.
> But for reasons known only to himself Bufano seems unwilling to
> bring this intellectual integrity into his other fields of endeavor.
>
> For example, Bufano's captious criticism of the San Francisco Sym-
> phony as well as his constant demand for what he calls a 50-cent
> symphony, do not take into consideration any of the existing cir-
> cumstances. Worse, Bufano repeatedly has been told the actual
> story and has been supplied with figures which he ignores.

Bufano didn't ignore figures; he didn't believe them. He
fought more tenaciously than ever and saw that his ideas were
beginning to take hold. The Art Commission music committee
recommended that the city sponsor at least two free symphony
concerts for service men. This came about only after Benny had
asked the various commandants of nearby military camps and
the service organizations to send letters suggesting such concerts.

Benny kept plugging. He requested $100,000 for a tree-plant-
ing program and "for the advancement of painting, sculpture,
and literature." He forgot none of the arts. His suggestion was
referred to a committee and the vote was seven-to-seven, but
Benny had fought his way up from a fourteen-to-one minority
to even Stephen.

He lost the next game, however, by seven-to-four. Bufano
wanted $20,000 to subsidize master artists in beautifying public
buildings, but Benny's old nemesis put in his two votes against
him. Only two, since Bufano had been successful in taking one
of Fleishhacker's three votes away from him. Benny had been
told that he should be nice to this man, because he had given
over a million dollars to the city.

"Yes, with strings attached," said Bufano, "so he can use all
you good people as my brother Remo manipulates his marion-
ettes."

The response to this was that all Bufano had given the people was some questionable art "and headaches every time we
meet."

"Headaches are a symptom of something wrong in your head. Maybe you're thinking too hard on how to outwit me. Let's relax."

Not only did Bufano make contacts with people in all parts of the United States, but he deluged people all over the world with letters. He wrote to President Truman and suggested that a new member of the cabinet be created. "I believe," he said in the letter, "that the American people are now ready to ask the United States Government about the possibility of creating in Washington, D.C., a Minister of Fine Arts. . . . It is a fact that all other civilized countries of the world, such as France, England, Italy, Russia, China, Mexico and all our sister countries of South America have a Minister of Fine Arts as a member of their cabinet." He had convincing reasons as to why the United States should have such an office, "but no one had ever done anything about it. I can't really understand why not. We've got every other kind of cabinet member, but not one interested in developing our culture and art."

Bufano, never forgetful of what Mayor Lapham had done for him, regularly wrote him letters of thanks, suggestions and reminders. In one of these letters, summarizing briefly some of his accomplishments, Benny said:

Dear Mayor Lapham:

For many years I have worked long and hard on a program to make this city more beautiful and more conscious of its great destiny.

This program includes the planting of trees in our streets, the placing of works of Art where they may be seen by busy working people, and not less of importance — the bringing of great music within the reach of all — through the medium of popular-priced symphonies.

This program has achieved national and international prominence — not because of me, but because of the underlying principle, namely — that beauty, art, and music are not the exclusive hobby of the wealthy — but *belong* to and must be placed within the *convenient* reach of all the people.

You, Mr. Mayor, by appointing me to the San Francisco Art Commission . . . by introducing me as your co-guest at the Press Club last year . . . by act, word, and deed . . . have endorsed my program.

This program is now beginning to function. The Art Commission
has recommended the planting of trees in the streets; and some
works of art are now being temporarily publicly displayed. Good!
But not good enough.

Next on the program is the People's Symphony, definitely scheduled for May 10, 12, and 13, one of which is to be a free concert
for the Armed Forces and their escorts.

The People's Symphony! Bufano had placed great hope in
this symphony. It was to be a test case against the smug com-
placency of big city bosses, art critics and doubting Thomases
of all kinds. Benny put everything he had into making it a success: he was able to get Sir Thomas Beecham to come from
London for the event and persuaded one of his friends to put
up the cash to back the costs. Other friends volunteered to build
up the program by advertising it, but Benny did not know it
would be done à la Hollywood.

Sir Thomas Beecham arrived in San Francisco ready to con-
duct three concerts. But the proud upper crust of San Francisco was chagrined at what was called the "circus" Benny had
planned. Music critic Alfred Frankenstein was the spokesman:
"He [Bufano] gathered together a helter-skelter ensemble and
then had sound trucks bark the distinguished name of Sir Thomas
Beecham through the streets as though he were a strip tease
dancer! The whole thing certainly did not contribute anything
to the career of this wonderful conductor!"

"Hell, he's too big a man to worry about contributing to his
career! We were having a big party for him at the Press Club!"
was Bufano's answer. Benny had pictures of the party, with
Beecham smiling broadly and drinking a toast to the success of
the concert, and Benny, a Cheshire grin on his face, his eyes
sparkling his triumph and happiness!

Afterward Frankenstein grudgingly admitted: "One cannot
escape the conclusion that [these] concerts did attract a size-
able, immensely appreciative and enthusiastic group not ordinarily served by the San Francisco Symphony."

Bufano, pleased that "there was not a mink coat in the house,"
was unhappy that his sponsor had lost about $10,000. "It can

all be turned into a profit the minute the ermine and mink circle stops playing politics and stops boycotting art for the people's sake." Benny was stalemated: in a way he had won, but in a way he had lost. The common people had not backed him up as he had thought they would. "I made mistakes, we all did, but I'm sure if we could do it now, it would be the greatest success ever." The opportunity to prove his point did not come.

In the next two months certain members of the Art Commission did everything to squelch Benny, but without success. Then suddenly the commission rushed through a regulation authorizing only its secretary to prepare, plan or release publicity on official activities of the Art Commission.

"That's a gag rule," yelled Benny. "Are you afraid to have your linen blowing in the public wind? Believe me, this commission is worse than the Gestapo! I want to know who's opening my personal mail. I've tried to get some concerts and ballets for service men, but you clucks block every move to help them. Now, when I get letters from Mare Island, Fort Ord, the Coast Guard, Fort Mason, the Naval Hospital at Oakland, and from the Office of the Commandant of the Navy, I find my mail opened for me. Why don't you use the steam system of mail opening? It would be much better and less annoying than the present crude methods."

The only reply was: "Pipe down, Benny. We've got more important business to talk about."

In Mayor Lapham's office Bufano told his side of the story. "That's your job, Benny," the mayor told him. "You're on there to fight for what you think is right. To me you've done more in six months than has ever been done before by all art commissioners collectively. I want you to stay on."

"Thanks, Mr. Mayor. I was going to hand in my resignation, but I'll stay and fight it out."

Benny's decision to stay on the commission helped make a change in the attitude of people toward him, but most of all it seemed that his dogged determination was beginning to have an effect where it would do the most good.

One of the members of the Board of Supervisors soon recommended that Benny's sculptures be placed in some public place, where all could enjoy them. The supervisor added, "Bufano's collection is magnificent, particularly the animal pieces, the seals, bears and cubs, frog, fish, cat and mouse, etc. They would give enjoyment especially to the youngsters of the city if they were in Union Square or some prominent place like that." The supervisor had learned that all the Bufano statues, nearly one hundred of them, finished or in various stages of completion, were in a shed in Sutro Forest, exposed to the weather, in danger of fire and threatened by all other forms of destruction. Some of them already had been chipped and otherwise damaged. The supervisor felt this was a shame, since Bufano was one of the great artists of our time.

Many other artists throughout San Francisco demanded a show of their own works, if Bufano was going to have a show. But before any exhibit was held, Bufano set the Art Commission on its ear again. This time a single word did it, and it was no swear word. At one of the meetings, Bufano proposed another charter amendment to reduce the commission to six members, with the mayor and chief administrative officer as ex-officio members. He was sure they'd have a much more effective organization if they had one painter, one architect, one writer, one businessman as a lay member, one sculptor and "a musicologist."

"A what!" bellowed the member representing the musician's union.

"A musicologist," Benny had answered, "but I hardly expected him to know what that meant. Any musician would know.

" 'Just what is a musicologist, Mr. Bufano?' he asked me.

"I explained that a musicologist understands all the various forms of music and is not just a violin or trumpet player. Such a man would have the broadest knowledge of the field, including its history. As I was talking, the president of the Library Commission walked out of the room and soon returned, glaring.

" 'Mr. Bufano,' he said, 'I think you're a liar and a deceiver. Furthermore, only crazy men invent or coin words. There's no such word in any dictionary.'

"I answered that it was probably because he couldn't spell. I told him to call the information desk in his own library, and they would be able to tell him what the word means without any trouble.

"He said he would do just that, just to show me up for what I really am. However, he wanted the president of our commission to do the calling and repeat word for word what the librarian told him over the phone. We might get a more objective report that way. The call was made and the president repeated the words to the commissioners.

" 'The word musicology,' said the president, 'is found in the unabridged dictionary, 1941 edition, and is defined as a branch of knowledge or field of investigation, especially the historical study of musical documents, investigation of sources, gathering and organization of neglected data.' "

Bufano, triumphant, walked out the door, followed by reporters. He led them to a dictionary and there pointed out the word for all to see. "I was right," said Benny. "He couldn't spell."

In the following year, 1946, Bufano was able to institute another of his ideas. Instead of the artist paying to show his work, he was to be paid for his exhibit. Bufano's work, not exhibited before, was shown with the works of other artists in the restaurant of Esther and Fenner Fuller in Oakland. Leon Liebes and Harry Camp extended the courtesy of lending the Bufano works which they owned to the show.

When Benny was asked to explain a poster he made entitled *United We Survive* he said: "The eagle in the background is the American eagle, the main figure just in front of the eagle with outstretched hands [reminiscent of St. Francis] is humanity; then in front of that, all of the human race is portrayed in small figures, some only represented by the eyes. This is my way of expressing that until we become a united humanity we will never have peace."

"When did you make the poster?" asked Fenner Fuller.

"I made it in the Aleutians when I first got into the war in 1942."

"But I thought you were a peaceful man, Benny, and a really true, peaceful man would have become a conscientious objector."

"That's what you think. . . . If I had objected, do you think the war would be any different?"

"Probably not, but when you were a young boy you cut off your trigger finger as a protest against war."

"Sure, but I've learned a lot since then. I still protest, but I don't do it alone. All my art, all my work aids me in putting my protests to work by showing the foolishness of war and the glories of peace. I went to war because I am an American and because our country was attacked. I'm not of a faith that preaches the theory of conscientious objection to war."

"Benny," Fuller said, "let's finish hanging up your pictures. This whole show is your idea, so you can have the choice wall for a better display of your work."

"What do you mean?" yelled Benny. "You ought to know me better than that!"

"Don't get excited, Benny. I was just trying to get a rise out of you! And I got it.

Bufano's reputation for truthfulness and a sense of fair play was perhaps his most highly prized possession; however, Christmas of 1946 was not far off when he received a jolt. Under the headline "Bufano is No Good," the *San Francisco Skylight,* a weekly journal of the arts, accused him of taking advantage of his position as chairman of the purchasing committee for the Municipal Art Exhibit. The journal charged that he had bought "works of art from his friend"; that in at least one case he had tried to purchase a work that had not even appeared in the show; and that he was attempting to buy extremely costly paintings from close personal friends. Bufano was not dismayed. "Nothing but a bunch of artists who became jealous of my accomplishments."

In 1948, a new mayor came on the scene, and Bufano went off the Art Commission. "I did my job as best I could," said Benny. "Of course I got in trouble, but the only guy who doesn't is the one who doesn't do anything. I'll always be active, come what may, but no matter what happens, I'll never give up on my principles."

16 ⸴ "One World" in a Cafeteria

Bufano said that many times an artist dies by the hands of his friends, but he is often resurrected by the sting of his enemies. "The most powerful possession in life is a true friend," he said. "I, personally, never lose a moment's sleep by the snares and contraptions put up by enemies, but my friends share a large part of my sleep." Benny had certainly been stung by his enemies while he served as art commissioner, but he also had many friends in San Francisco who wished him well. Ted Wettland was one of these.

David W. Moar, a bustling West Coast restaurateur, wanted to have a cafeteria with his own name on it. Wettland, who designed cafeterias and who, years before, had studied art under Bufano, suggested that Moar go whole hog in the decoration of this cafeteria and have a Bufano photo mural on one large wall.

Benny's version of the story is as follows:

"Wettland told Moar that I was the only man for the job. Moar called me at the Press Club. The press boys had given me a room in the club to live in. I was, and am, always poorer than the proverbial church mouse; so I guess they felt sorry for me.

"When he called me, Moar said he was in the restaurant business and was building a new cafeteria on Powell Street. He said he wanted to talk to me about doing a mural on one of the walls. I answered it was lucky he got me because I was just about to leave for a trip to Lambaréné, in Africa. I wanted to talk to Dr. Schweitzer about peace.

"Moar asked me to have lunch with him that day. I put on my best suit, the one made of the cloth I wove when I was with Gandhi years before. At the lunch I ordered cottage cheese, a

183

plate of fruit and a glass of buttermilk. Moar and Wettland
ordered steak sandwiches and coffee. Typical American food.
Moar plunged into the matter of the mural, saying he wanted
a photo mural to go on one big wall of the dining room.

"I told him I couldn't see why he wanted a photo mural. Why
not have a mosaic that would have a functional as well as artistic
value?" Until Benny met Moar, he had never attempted a mosaic,
a comparatively obsolete art form. The flamboyant tile jobs seen
in modern buildings were not what Bufano considered mosaics.
To him, mosaics meant the magnificent decorations of Saint
Sophia in Istanbul, Saint Mark's in Venice and the churches at
Ravenna. Made of tesserae — colored marble for floors and colored glass for walls and ceilings — these were the real mosaics.

"Moar looked at Ted Wettland a little skeptically and wondered if it wouldn't be pretty expensive. I asked him if he was
thinking of expenses or a work of art. All he wanted was to
decorate the dining room, something suitable to a restaurant,
like fish, ducks, chickens, loaves of bread, roasting pigs and things
like that. I told him immediately that I knew how to cook but
I wasn't looking for a job as a cook. I was pretty peeved by the
suggestion. I told him if he wanted a work of art he'd have to
leave it to me. If not, he could get another man for the job.
I hate the thought of a pig roasted whole. It's barbarous. I was
a vegetarian at that time.

"Ted Wettland tried to calm me by telling me not to get
excited. We could talk the matter over calmly.

"Mr. Moar had calmed down by this time and asked me what
subject I thought we should use for the mosaic.

"Quick as a flash I answered, 'St. Francis.' I guess Wettland
was thinking about the controversy over the saint for Twin Peaks
because he looked like he'd been hit by a chunk of marble. Moar
looked like he was about to have a seizure of apoplexy; he yelled
out, 'St. Francis? What the hell has St. Francis got to do with
a cafeteria?'

"I got hot under the collar and started pounding on the
table and yelled back, 'To hell with your cafeteria! That's not
important!'

"Moar told me in no uncertain terms that the cafeteria was damned important to him. And besides he was going to pay for the mosaic.

"So I cooled down and told him if that's the way he felt, we might as well forget the whole thing. No hard feelings.

"Ted Wettland tried to pacify both of us and said we could talk it over calmly. I answered that there was nothing to talk about.

"A week went by and I guess Moar fought the thing out with himself. He finally called me up again at the Press Club. I was in the bathroom so I guess I didn't answer the phone as fast as I should. When I finally did, Moar sounded relieved. He yelled into the phone, 'Damn it! Where the hell were you? I thought you'd gone off to Africa. Can you meet me for lunch today?'

"'Sure, I'll meet you at the St. Francis,'* I told him. He sounded kind of stunned: the name acted peculiarly on him.

"At the St. Francis I noticed that Moar ordered cottage cheese and a plate of fresh fruit. I advised him to have a glass of buttermilk. He did but he looked kind of sick. I guess he never in his life had a glass of buttermilk before. Maybe gin was more to his liking.

"I told Moar that I had been thinking about that mosaic and I got a swell idea for it. Moar looked hopeful; maybe the poor guy thought I had forgotten about St. Francis. So I went on saying that they could mount the mosaic on a portable wooden flat, framed in stainless steel, so it could be taken out of the cafeteria. Moar almost split a gut at this idea."

Bufano went on, "I told him I was planning the mosaic for the United Nations. Meanwhile it could be placed in his cafeteria until such time as the United Nations accepted it. I told Moar his name would go down in history. He got pale at this idea. It seemed he wasn't at all sure that he wanted his name to go down in history. All he wanted was a decoration for his cafeteria.

"This was okay with me. I told him we'd have one of the greatest works of art of the century on that wall, and then I

*St. Francis Hotel.

asked him when I could go to Italy. He was flabbergasted. What the hell did I have to go to Italy for? I explained that I'd have to go to get the tesserae; the only place in the world where they made them was Italy — either at the Vatican or in Venice. That's where the kilns are for the firing of the mosaic stone.

"Mr. Moar looked beaten down, and wanted to know how long it would take to get the stones.

"I told him I couldn't be sure. Maybe a year.

"Moar said rather grimly that this thing had to be finished for the opening. And how much money would it take?

"I told him I thought about $20,000.

"He almost fell off his chair and asked if I make them out of gold. I explained that some of them have gold in them."

Bufano submitted sketches which Moar, under the tender guidance of Wettland, approved. He gave Bufano a letter of credit for $15,000, not even asking him to sign anything. Benny was delighted.

Originally, he had intended to do all his work in Italy, but Moar had attached one rider to the commission: Bufano had to have the mural finished by the end of April, 1950, for the opening of the new Moar's Cafeteria. When Benny discovered that a place in St. Louis imported tesserae from Italy, he went there and put together two of the three panels. But after two panels, he ran out of colors, particularly yellow, so he went to Italy anyway. There he bought the rest of the mosaics and hired additional workmen to assemble the final panel. While in Europe, Bufano wrote Moar asking for an additional $5,000. It was sent. Moar had spent $35,000 or more, when he had only planned on a thousand or so for the photo mural. The mosaic was completed and hung in time for the gala opening of the cafeteria.

When the mural was finally finished Moar said he felt that Bufano had done the work only for the sake of art. The artist had made no monetary gain at all.

"I came out about even," said Bufano. "That Moar is a really wonderful guy. He gave me a gold pass to eat at his cafeteria free for the rest of my life!"

Bufano's mosaics, each panel measuring 16 feet 4 inches high and 14 feet wide, are set in mortar against huge, removable stainless-steel trays. He used, in all, 7000 shades. The design is in some ways reminiscent of the poster *United We Survive*. In one panel he shows the children of the various races under the protective arms of a large figure entitled Humanity, which in turn is topped by a great eagle. In the center panel all racial groups merge into one figure as the peace is signed. In the third, peace becomes a fact with St. Francis of Assisi hovering benignly over singing birds and a peaceful wolf.

Benny explained that these mosaics "represent the union of the past and the present under the aegis of peace. I chose children for the mosaics because they are closest to the Deity in their attributes of innocence, simplicity and brotherhood. They act true to nature in the love and association with all other children, whether in play or study, in games or enterprise. Their hearts know no man-made guile or treachery. Their experiences know no man-made prejudice, hate, war and destruction. That is why the Bible glorifies the child when it says, 'A child shall lead them.' That is why the Bible exalts the example of the child when it says, 'Ye shall not enter the Kingdom of Heaven, unless you become little children.'"

The colors Benny used in the children's groups "represent the three major groupings of the human race . . . the white, the black and the yellow. Refinements in color show the variations of peoples within the three groupings.

"The palms of the children's hands are open because children are frank and open in their relations among themselves, knowing no underhanded stratagems and frauds. In the language of the scriptures, they most nearly fill the requirements to ascend unto the hill of the Lord, because they have clean hands and a pure heart, and have not sworn deceitfully.

"Some of the children have one eye. The one eye is a symbol for the oneness of creation, the oneness of destiny. The one eye reduces to the utmost simplicity the idea that our mortality, with all its problems and interests, binds us together as one to work for the common good. That is why the child's right hand is seen signing a pact of peace. That is why the child's left hand clasps the United Nations covenant as an instrument of hope.

"The colors of the mosaic, like creation, are blended into a rich and lively harmony. The child standing on the horizon in a burst of light symbolizes the refreshed hope that comes with birth and the buoyant adventure that lies with the future. The light of bright colors suggests the knowledge, love and unity that lift men from the tragic darkness of ignorance, superstition and baseness.

"The female child at the top of the mosaic is a little older, a little more mature, and a little more aware than the others, she senses and slightly broods over the imperfections that threaten the oneness, the unity, the peace and the destiny of humanity.

"The eagle represents the United States soaring on the wings of man's highest flights in imagination: liberty, equality and happiness. It is one of the noblest experiments of government to give all men, regardless of the accidents of birth, the opportunity and incentive to find their rightful place in society, based on character and talent. It projects a new dignity and destiny for the common man as a member of the state's sovereign power.

"The St. Francis is a symbol of peace. He knew cosmic creation as one. Accordingly, he was friend to man and animal: the birds felt no timidity in his presence; the wolf lost his ferocity; man was the object of his solicitude. Because St. Francis has transferred to the wolf his sense of oneness of creation, I have put the wolf at the feet of the saint. The wolf no longer feels alien and hostile to the townspeople of Gubbio, of which he was once the predatory terror, but now feels a community of interest and the blessing of peace. In fact, he is now the benign mascot of the town. This suggests a kinship to the Biblical prophecy of the lion lying down with the lamb, and swords being turned into ploughshares and spears into pruning hooks.

"In all, the mosaic represents the symbol of 'one world.' The children symbolize the oneness of human creation and the unity of man — the fatherhood of God and the brotherhood of man. They oppose man's inhumanity to man. They protest fratricide, the murder of brother by brother in savage warfare. They proclaim the principle that only the Deity, who gives life, can take life."

The mosaic was completed and safely housed in the cafeteria, where no vandals could destroy it. But, inside Benny was always the memory of his twelve-ton statue of St. Francis, lying for 28 years in a far corner of a Paris warehouse, looking like a cadaver shrouded in dusty gunny sacks.

17 ' The Wandering Saint

Before Bufano finished his mosaics he gave "that great guy Moar" many hours of anxiety and frustration. Someone played a joke on Moar and wrote him from South America, saying that Benny had just been seen driving a Rolls Royce with two beautiful blondes along the Rio streets. Actually Bufano was busy shuttling back and forth from Italy, and while in Italy he had become inspired with putting the story of Joseph and Mary in mosaics.

"I had thought about it for a long time, but it wasn't until I got to Italy that things began to take form. Back in San Francisco, while other workmen were finishing up my mosaics for Moar, I started on an idea that I thought was as revolutionary as my stainless steel. It was what I called 'mosaics in the round.' Instead of making flat mosaics, I curved them around the body, the arms or whatever else was three-dimensional." The statues were wood carvings, 10 feet 6 inches high and weighing a half ton each. Benny had used fifty differently colored stones in each mosaic. St. Joseph has the Christ child at his feet, while the Virgin Mary holds the infant Christ in her arms.

For a long time these beautiful creations lay in the basement of the Stanford University Museum, waiting to be put on display. Seeing his statues in such a lowly state, Bufano became angry, and the image of his *St. Francis de La Varenne* in the Paris warehouse returned to him. In 1936 he had tried to present the statue to San Francisco, but without success. No one wanted to pay for its passage from Paris.

"They can all go to hell, everybody in this city," screamed Bufano. "For years I've been trying to give San Francisco my statue of *St. Francis of Varenne*. Maybe that was a mistake. Maybe if I'd tried to sell it I would have gotten somewhere."

It was in 1955 that Bufano's dream finally came true. He offered the statue to the church of St. Francis of Assisi at Columbus Avenue and Vallejo Street. The Reverend Alvin Wagner, pastor of the church, accepted the gift, and the church paid Benny's passage to France to supervise the packing and shipping of the statue. With the aid of art patrons and benefactors of the church, the sculpture was redeemed from storage for a thousand dollars and arrangement was made with the French Line to ship the St. Francis free of charge.

When Father Wagner went to the water-front warehouse to see the crates opened for inspection, he found the statue in perfect condition. He also discovered that the thrifty, opportunistic Bufano had tucked his bag of sculptor's tools and some other smaller sculptures into the crates. The good father overlooked this bit of chicanery with a smile.

The statue was officially dedicated October 4, 1955; to his horror Benny found that the name of only one out of a dozen or more women who had collected money for the St. Francis project was carved into the stone of the pedestal. He was indignant. He went to Father Wagner and protested, telling him it was not fair; either all the women's names must be put on the pedestal or this one name must come off.

The pastor tried to explain that this woman had done a great deal of the work. Finally, he said he would see what could be done. Bufano gave him two weeks to get the name off the statue.

The newspapers got hold of the story and blew it up. One paper came out with a story that this wealthy woman had given Bufano $7500. Benny became furious and said he had never received one lousy buck. In his room in the Press Club, he lay awake fuming and fretting over the injustice. Sleep would not come to him, but indignation did. Finally he could stand it no longer; he dressed, went to his studio for a chisel and hammer, then went to the church, where his St. Francis stood on the steps, hands outstretched in benediction. Bufano chiseled off the offending name.

Later that year Bufano got a notice from the Internal Revenue Service demanding to know why he hadn't paid taxes on the $7500 he had received for the statue *St. Francis of Varenne.* Bufano wrote on the back of the letter: "If you can find that seventy-five hundred, you're welcome to keep seventy hundred and give me the five."

The *St. Francis of Varenne* stood on the steps of the church from 1955 until November, 1960, when the Reverend John J. Curtin replaced Father Wagner. Mr. Curtin had never liked the statue and claimed it interferred with the weddings and funeral processions going in and out of the church.

Of all the Catholic churches in San Francisco, there wasn't one that would welcome Bufano's saint. Where to put the statue became the issue of the day, and Bufano's action in chiseling out the lone name on the pedestal more than ever made the parishioners take sides. There were violent discussions at homes, at work and even in the church. St. Francis, the patron saint of peace, was inadvertently involved in at first a skirmish, then a battle. In order to prevent a war, Father Curtin decided to do something about it.

In a three-column spread, including a cut of the beneficent St. Francis with children staring up at his benign face, the *New York Times* (November 27, 1960) stated:

> Beniamino Benvenuto Bufano is a five foot, 120 pound sculptor who fashions stone and metal, notably black granite and stainless steel, into colossi.
>
> He also creates controversies to match his statues.
>
> In the vortex of as lively a public outcry as "Benny" ever presided over, is his heroic (12 feet high and 16 tons) statue of the gentle St. Francis. It is one of a dozen such statues of St. Francis that the sculptor has conceived or brought to stages of completion.
>
> This cruciform version, hewn entirely from black Swedish granite, stands with arms outstretched on the steps of St. Francis of Assisi Church, the city's second oldest, in the North Beach district.
>
> It has stood there five years, delighting citizens who regard Bufano as a genius, infuriating those who hold that he is a cantankerous trouble-maker and that his works are monstrosities.

It will not stand there much longer. That is the decree of the Rev.
John J. Curtin, pastor of the church, who announced this week
that he had consulted with the Archdiocese and that this St. Francis would have to go.

Bufano suggested the Civic Center for his statue. Mayor
George Christopher politely declined the offer. Arguments and
invectives tormented the peace of the city. Finally Maynard
Corlett of Oakland became enamored of the St. Francis. He
wanted it for Oakland, but Bufano rejected his offer. Nevertheless the indefatigable Corlett, determined to help, contacted
people in Oakland, San Francisco, Los Angeles and Pasadena,
trying to find a place for the statue.

Cities other than Oakland welcomed Benny with reservations.
For instance, on May 14, 1961, the *Independent Star-News* of
Pasadena remarked that the city should "Beware of Bufano."

Pasadena had better brace itself. Benny Bufano is here.

The mighty little man of sculpture, who loves to make statues 20
feet tall and stands only five feet high himself, has a habit of
creating a controversy as well as carvings, wherever he goes. He
visited Pasadena's City Hall recently. He cast a calculating eye
around it. This may mean that he is about to offer a statue to the
city. If so, and if the past repeats, such an offer could shatter the
peace of Pasadena.

Last month Bufano threw San Francisco and Oakland into an uproar that echoed all over the Bay Area, involved two city halls,
several art museums, newspapers, television, radio, and any number of angry and adoring citizens.

The scrappy little sculptor, whose studio is in San Francisco's
North Point Sewage Treatment Plant and whose work stands in
the Metropolitan Museum of Art, has never been silenced by
criticism. He once remarked in public that San Francisco's Mayor,
George Christopher, reminded him of a "modern Pilate washing
his hands at the Crucifixion." That remark was made during Bufano's latest battle, over his statue of St. Francis.

When word got out that the church didn't want the saint, a group
of Bufano buffs started a campaign to get the granite moved to a
park in Oakland. . . . One resident there said in public meeting,
"I'm suspicious of anything that San Francisco wants to give
Oakland."

In the midst of the controversy a church member sued his priest
in court for giving the priceless religious art treasure away. San

Francisco columnist Herb Caen was moved to write a poem about the battle. Objections to the St. Francis statue were both religious and artistic. "Send it to the Pope!" said one anonymous letter-writer, and others said, "Not in a public park. Let's keep religion in the church!"

On artistic grounds the statue was attacked as "hideous!" "It should be towed out to sea on a barge and thrown overboard," said one commentator, and others called it "a cartoon in concrete" and said, "send it to Disneyland, where it would be at home among the imitation jungles and the pseudo Matterhorn."

Yet many sound businessmen and institutions wrote letters welcoming the statue to Oakland. These included Coldwell, Banker and Company ("an attractive and significant work of art") . . . . the Oakland Art Museum, the American Institute of Architects ("a great work of art") . . . . and the Warehousemen's Union ("we are just ordinary working people but we know what pleases our senses").

Bufano finally succeeded in getting the money to move the statue, and *St. Francis of Varenne* was moved to private property in the business section of Oakland. A picture of Benny (*Los Angeles Mirror,* March 15, 1961) atop the extended arm of his St. Francis shows him placing a bouquet of roses on his beloved statue. Symbolic? Everything about his art is symbolic, and the roses were probably a hope on Bufano's part that this would end the "stink" over his St. Francis.

Ten weeks later the property was rented to Pan American Airways, which found that the statue obstructed the entrance to the building. *St. Francis of Varenne* had to move again, and it was moved to Si's Charbroiler in Oakland. The good saint blessed the people eating giant hamburgers. Simon Furman, the owner of the hamburger place, said that his business had increased and some people came to kneel at the feet of the saint.

Finally Bufano's friends in the International Longshoreman's Union came to a decision to place the statue in front of the I.L.W.U. Memorial Hall near Fisherman's Wharf in San Francisco. Bufano was delighted. In December, 1962, the I.L.W.U. brought the sculpture back to the city. At a cost of $3000 St. Francis was installed in a small plaza near the water front. Benny was happy then, but doubt crept in and he said: "Possibly this time St. Francis will stay put, but only time will tell."

18 ' The Man of Stature

In 1958, the International Geophysical Year, *Sputnik* was launched and the world was yelling for peace. In a wave of cultural exchanges, movie stars, students and tourists were headed for the Soviet Union to peek behind the Iron Curtain. Benny, the ever-watchful, saw a chance for the fruition of his life's ambition. For many years Benny had dreamed of seeing a Bufano statue in front of the United Nations Building in New York.

Bufano's belief was that the artist is mankind's most economical ambassador of good will. He is equipped with the basic language of the universe. God blessed him with a will to survive and an endless, roving desire to watch his fellow man. Bufano not only wanted to watch his fellow man, but he wanted to sell peace, peace at any price.

"Peace is not something you shout from the rooftops," said Benny. "It's not something you preach. It's something you live. Peace is a fighting word. You have to believe in it hard enough to give your life for it. To me, humanity is a wonderful thing. If we believed in other people, if we trusted them, wars would be on the way out."

Russia had heard about the great sculptor — and knew of his peace plan. Since 1958 was the fortieth anniversary of the Russian Revolution, and since cultural exchange was popular, Bufano received an invitation to come for the celebration. He had peace on his mind, and also a four-foot model of *Peace* in his arms.

"When I arrived in Moscow, they asked me what I wanted to see the most. All the other guys I was with from the United States wanted to see their schools, their legal institutions, and their industrial and agricultural programs at work. Me? I said I wanted to see Premier Bulganin. They sort of laughed at me, thinking maybe I was kidding. I wasn't."

More than a week later, at one of the remote schools he was visiting, Bufano was urgently requested to answer a phone call. "It was from Bulganin himself," he said. "Everybody around me was sort of dumbstruck to think that he would call me. I was thrilled myself. I couldn't imagine Eisenhower calling me personally, or even a visiting artist. So Bulganin invited me to visit him."

Bufano brought his model of *Peace* along with him when he went to see Bulganin. "He was a great guy," Benny said with his usual hyperbole. "He listened to everything I had to say. He thought my model was great but said he didn't think they could put up a four-hundred-foot statue of it, as it might take up too much space. He suggested that they could shoot it to the moon for me, and I'd be the first sculptor on the moon. He told me that my concept of peace was too simple; that peace was much more complex than I had represented it; that I had better start talking peace to Eisenhower; and that when Eisenhower and Dulles were ready, he was ready. He said that maybe I, as an artist, could be instrumental in bringing the two countries together. Bulganin gave me a special message to bring to President Eisenhower. I told him I would deliver it personally."

As to the statue for the United Nations, Bulganin informed Bufano that the Soviet Union had its own sculptors who could make a peace statue. They wouldn't be very apt to commission an artist from the United States. He hoped that Bufano would understand this.

"When I got back to San Francisco I sent a telegram to President Eisenhower, asking for an interview."

One week later Bufano received the answer saying, "Communication from the heads of recognized governments to the President are normally forwarded through regular diplomatic channels, and it would not be customary or proper for the President to receive such communications through a private third party."

Immediately, Bufano sat down and drafted his answer to the White House in a bitter letter expressing his feelings about this refusal. He said later: "Some of the things we do and don't do in this country drive me crazy. It's not that I wasn't personally permitted to see Eisenhower, it's that they just dismiss the common man. They don't give a damn about the average man except for his vote.

"I was not only an average man but I am a little man in size. Many times people pass me by without seeing me. They're not accustomed to looking down at a little guy, not much more than five feet tall. Years ago I used to be quite sensitive, thinking that people were ignoring me as they held their heads high in the air and whisked by me. In a world of giants — I mean all people five-feet-five and over — it's kind of tough for a little guy to make himself recognized. Lots of them have done it though. Napoleon was one; Mayor La Guardia of New York was another. And in all due modesty, I'm another.

"Psychologists call this compensation and when it's overdone they call it overcompensation. Well and good. The point is . . . because I have made great big statues, such as Sun Yat-sen, St. Francis, the statue of Peace . . . have I been compensating or overcompensating for my miniature stature? I don't see that it makes much difference. I'm doing something, that's the important thing. Yes, I have made big things and I will continue to do so. To me, there are several simple reasons why I make them big. One is that they don't get lost so easily. Another is, that a big statue can be put in a commanding location and can act as a landmark. Another reason is that it becomes practically indestructible. Finally, I like to work on something big, it challenges me."

And he *was* working on something big, a colossal hand for the C.I.O. Union Building. In order to reduce costs, Benny chose to work in copper and mosaics, rather than stainless steel or granite. The hand is executed simply, each joint and finger being represented by the most basic geometric forms; circles and ellipses. The thumb is in the same plane with the four fingers, so that the palm is flattened, accentuating the mosaic design of the children of the world. The hand is greatly stylized; it is massive rather than detailed, more a representation of the strength of labor united than a replica of a human hand.

Benny had never made any pretense that his works were exact replicas of anything at all. "That wouldn't be art, that would be photography," he often said. His bears might look like seals and a mouse like a pig, but it wasn't what they looked like that was important. "It's what they feel like to children, it's what they symbolize to children, it's what adults can perceive, too, if they only free themselves from their restrictions and limited adult concepts.

"Art needs to be simple. Its origins must come from the earth, from the people themselves. I am reminded of the *Saturday Evening Post* story about me on January 21, 1961."

On a two-page spread in the *Post* was a delightful, tender story about how elementary-school children prevailed upon Benny — and the powers that be — to have him cast an eight and a half ton granite statue of a bear for their school. And the *Post* stated: "A chain reaction of enthusiasm . . . eventually engulfed the whole student body and a good part of the community." Benny donated the casting and his artistic labor, while the community with "spaghetti dinners and ice-cream and bean-bag sales produced $1040 to pay for the materials and hauling."

Governor Edmund Brown of California, "teachers, parents, local dignitaries and nine hundred young bear-lovers of Heights Elementary were all on hand as the statue was unveiled." The *Post* story concluded: "Benny's bear may not look much like California's official grizzly, but to the kids it will always be a beautiful symbol of the wonders that work and determination can perform."

Bufano later said, "I liked that article in the *Post* very much. The writer showed so much more understanding of art and children than most of them who think that art criticism or stories should be snide and satirical. I realize that I'm the type of guy who invites wise-cracking rejoinders. I can be pretty insulting at times, quite a jokester. And I'm aware that journalists lead me on. I'm good copy, as the boys say.

"The *Post* article said that I 'love children and that children love his sensitive and exquisitely beautiful sculptures of children, yet he refuses to acknowledge a child whom his divorced wife says is his.' All this is true, but I can't answer it in full here. This story has been told in many ways but I have the true story tucked away and hidden from public view. There are things in one's life that must remain forever within the soul of a man.

"In an article that appeared in *Newsweek*, they had a picture of me working in my studio, and there was a headline asking, 'Can Efficient Sewage Disposal Coexist with Art?' The story is simply that San Francisco had permitted me to temporarily use an unoccupied corner of one of the city's sewage treatment centers because I had no studio and needed space to work on an art commission for the city. As the story goes, I'm supposed to have worked diligently through the years, inching in more and more on space not otherwise used, until a recent inspection tour disclosed the fact that I had usurped a thousand square feet of the plant, and that it was impossible to move me out even if they wanted to, as I'd brought in tons and tons of granite and other huge stones and pieces of stainless steel to work upon.

"So what, is all I can say. I think it's better to use space than to leave it vacant. I didn't steal anything. I guess I just stayed longer than they expected, that's all. Which is what the article refers to when it closes with 'Benny is a great guy, but don't invite him for a weekend.'

"It's true that sometimes I extend my visits. But it's also true that I don't stay long enough sometimes. At least, people seem glad to see me when I come and sad to see me leave. If these people are putting on an act, then to hell with them. They are deceivers, and not worth having as friends. A guy in my position sometimes doesn't know what to do. It's hard to know what to make of people. I've been called everything under the sun. Benny the artist, they've called me. Benny the adventurer, the raconteur, the orator, the philosopher and writer, the actor, the comedian. And Benny the bum. Benny the moocher, Benny . . . the master of everything but tact.

"All of them are right. I'm a little bit of everything. I can't help what I am. And I don't want to change. I am a Christian, but I'm also a Jew. I am Christ, but I'm also Antichrist. I know myself pretty well. I have created great works of art, but I have also destroyed some of my great works. I am a peaceful man, but I know I have been mean, contemptible and even vicious. I have used and misused my friends. I have been an opportunist. I am impossible to pin down, and when it comes to having a contract with me, watch out. I don't like to be tied down. I don't like to have things spelled out. I like my freedom. I have lied. I have cheated. I have done many things I'm not proud of. What else should I admit? Anything and everything. I'm not afraid of saying anything. I'm not afraid to do anything. And for these things, I thank God. Above all else, despite all my sins, I know I am a great man. And I know I love mankind. I dedicate my life therefore to art, and peace, and the happiness of mankind. Join with me."

Bufano was a man who did not question the truth nor did he ever hesitate to voice it. In his later years, when he had learned something of himself and of the world, he was better able to cope with both triumph and adversity — at least in public.

Whenever Benny finished a piece of work he felt lost, as alone as when he had left Muriel in the nunnery. And, as always, in his hours of sorrow he spoke to her: "I feel like I did when you left me, Little Sister of the Stones." He glanced up at the crayoned quotation written in Italian on the plaster wall of the sewage plant: "When I begin my work I sing . . . when I come to the end, I die."

He wondered what would happen to his work; what would be his reward? Would he be honored for his beautiful and original pieces, or would San Francisco tear, smash, burn this treasure, the work of his hands? Would they be discarded to the dump pile or simply stay put in the sewage system? Bufano had learned, through the years, to laugh at vandalism and disappointment.

True, San Francisco had done its duty. Benny's statue of *Peace* was put up at the airport, and San Francisco had some of his other work placed inconspicuously about: in a housing project, in a park, in front of a church and in a cafeteria. The Hillsdale Shopping Center had eleven of his statues, and Stanford University had more of them buried in a basement, waiting to be exhibited. Yes, San Francisco had grudgingly put up some of his works. She had been lavish in her praise and merciless in her condemnation. It was always Hello, Benny . . . He's a swell little guy . . . His work's terrific . . . It's a monstrosity . . . I love that guy . . . I hate him . . . He's a bastard . . . He's wonderful . . . He's brave . . . He's nuts . . . He's got guts!

But the people of San Francisco had inflicted one wound so deep and so painful that Benny was forced to laugh to keep from crying: they had laughed at him again and again. And Benny laughed back, acted the clown. "And the whole world does nothing but laugh at me! No! It laughs at its own nothingness!"

Alone in his room at the Press Club or working like a madman in his studio, Benny did not laugh. Sometimes, when the world had been particularly rough on him, he would shove aside the accumulation of stuff on his table and sit down to pour out his bitterness in letters to the Little Sister of the Stones:

Everything laughed violently at me today. The sun laughed — the wind laughed — everything in the blue sky laughed — the hills, the trees, the valleys, every flower laughed and shed a few tears. And tonight a million pin points, a million laughs, light and clear night skies. Even the moon, a prostitute of a million years, with a million crimes in her belly, looks scornfully on, laughing in the loneliness of my thoughts. Everything in my studio quietly scolded me today — my tools, my stones, my drawings, my room, my Saint Francis, my Sun Yat-sen, everything laughed at me and so the whole day slowly laughed scornfully on.

There is every indication in the clear skies tonight that the sun and the blue, blue skies will carry on its laughing campaign on the morrow, laughing, laughing from rising to setting, and to relay its laughter to every star in the gray-blue sky in the long hours of night and dawn, and as I stand alone and gaze from my little room I see the whole of humanity laughing. The mob, a seething mob of gravediggers digging each other's graves at the accelerated pace of human greed and treachery. I thought I saw you in the mob of this sadness — this is the saddest. As for me, I hope I shall fall asleep tonight and sleep on to cheat the coming day!

Epilogue

BY HOWARD WILKENING

The psychiatrist Otto Rank claims that the artist and the neurotic have a "fundamental point in common: they have committed themselves to the pain of separation from the herd — that is, from unreflective incorporation of the views of their society. The path of the artist so committed is not an easy one, and he not infrequently resorts to neurotic maneuvers in order to maintain a necessary equilibrium. But the artist is essentially able to achieve an integration of his separate will and his need for union through a creative relationship to others."

On one occasion, Benny said: "Why do psychiatrists and psychologists make such an effort to explain the behavior of people? Why can't they let people alone, let them be? The more we try to intellectually understand ourselves, the further we get away from our true selves, the child in us.

"The child is such a wonderful being. Take a look at him the next time you can. I'm sure you'll find that the one thing that always brings mankind together is finding his own childhood in the other man. All creative people see themselves in the other artist — whether he be writer, sculptor, painter or musician. They're all basically a bunch of kids. As for scientists and mathematicians — they're a bunch of lost kids, denying their childhood. And some of them never find their child-selves again until they're old men — like Einstein and Max Planck — then they become philosophers and kids again."

Benny's world was one world, that of the child, the simplicity and genius of the child. To him, if we had child-geniuses running the world there would be no strife, no hatred, no war. As usual Benny paraphrased and personalized the ideas of an earlier philosopher when he said: "It's like Plato said, in a world like that, only peace would reign. I've been called a child, even a genius, and sometimes even worse. So, if I'm a child, I'm a genius; if I'm a genius, I'm a child. As one or the other I'll live and fight for Peace — until I die."

Child, genius, fighter for Peace, humble artist, egotist, revolutionary, realist, idealist, child — these were the masks of Bufano. Seldom did anyone peer behind these masks; never did anyone take his masks off. However, in a long association with Benny — as his friend, as his informal therapist, as his confidant — I learned many things about him, in a sense, when the mask slipped for a little while.

"Up until the time I met you," he told me one day, "never did I confide in anyone except my mother. Many times I wanted to reveal myself to Aubrey Williams, and I felt the same way about Henry Miller. But I always backed away from Henry at the last minute, yet I felt toward him the way I would have liked to have felt toward my father. One day I almost told him, when we were at his place in the Big Sur, that I had never purposely cut my trigger finger off.

"It was an accident. Ranieri had convinced me that to be a sculptor I would have to become ambidextrous. So I used my left hand whenever possible. One day, when sawing some wood, I hit a knot and the saw jumped and sliced my finger off clean, or at least through the bone. It scared the hell out of me, and I thought I was doomed as an artist. Dr. Tomasulo, the neighborhood doctor, was the one who gave me the idea about sending my finger to President Wilson.

" 'Doc,' I said, 'am I doomed? Will I be able to work anymore?'

"He sort of laughed at me. 'It's up to you,' he said. 'A determined man can overcome any handicap. Now, if you were a hunter I would say otherwise, unless you became lefty. With your trigger finger gone, you can't shoot, and it's the best excuse not to go to war.'

" 'Good,' I said, 'good. I'll make out. Doc, I want my finger, I've got an idea.'

"'You can have it, Beniamino,' he said, 'but you'll have to preserve it in alcohol, else it'll rot and stink.'

"'The stinkier the better,' I said, and later that day I mailed it to President Wilson. I think it cost me eight cents. But I think his front line of guys stopped it before it ever got to him, because when I spoke to Wilson later, he said he had never received it. He acted embarrassed, but he put on a smile and patted me on the shoulder. I think he felt sorry for me. Lots of people did, and I hated it. I used to feel sorry for myself, but a man can be and should be allowed that privilege."

Many of Benny's friends have called him a genius, others have called him brilliant but disorganized, while still others, not necessarily his friends, have labeled him a madman, psychotic, an idiot, a liar, cheat, damned with "a criminal's psychology," and a pervert. Typical of Benny, he said they were all telling some partial truths about him.

"I used to be ashamed of myself, I was so small. When La Guardia, the Little Flower, became mayor of New York, I was the happiest guy around. He was a shrimp like me, but he had more meat on him. I even had ideas that I could become a politician too. If I could have become mayor of San Francisco, it would have become the greatest art center in the world. I had crazy ideas, but I could have become mayor if things had gone right. A few guys got in my way — Fleishhacker was one — and sometimes the press twisted things around so that I must have looked pretty stupid to everybody. Donovan Bess was always fair, though, and so was Kevin Wallace. Herb Caen was marvelous. And so was Frankenstein. Lots of people were wonderful to me. And some were bastards.

"One of them was that guy at UCLA you introduced me to, back in 1948. You were a psychologist testing veterans for jobs. I asked you about the tests they were taking, and I remember saying that I would like to take them too, that I was a veteran. And you brought me into that room, and for hours that bastard of a guy asked me the most embarrassing questions.

"I went back three different times and the last time he gave me some vocational guidance. He said — I'll never forget it — that

I should probably work in civil service, maybe garbage collection, and that as a hobby I should take up some arts and crafts, although at my late age I would never get anywhere. The bastard. I knew you hadn't told him who I was. I even told you not to. That guy was so funny, the way he held those test results up to his chest so I couldn't see them.

"There's a little bit of thief in me, as you know, so when that guy turned around to answer the phone — he must have been on it for ten minutes — I swiped some papers from his folder. You never knew that, did you? Later, when I read and reread them, I laughed and laughed until I cried. But to be honest with you, I cried more than I laughed. I've always cried a lot in my life, mainly when things went against me. And when I'd stop hammering on my art to take a breath — that's when it would hit me that there was something wrong with my brain. And that's what that guy had found out with those tests — that inkblot test and the Wechsler Bellevue intelligence test, and so damned many others.

"He wrote that I probably had a brain lesion, that I was psychotic as well as almost feeble-minded. He used big words, but I went to the library and read and studied every word he mentioned. I was an expert after a while. He said that my I.Q. was 78, and because of the vast difference between my verbal scores and my performance scores I must have a lesion in my brain, to account for my psychotic responses. Hell, a guy with an I.Q. like that couldn't even be a garbage collector.

"I really fooled that guy. He asked me to name the capital of Italy, and so naturally I said Rawalpindi. Who wrote the Iliad, and I answered Rabindranath Tagore. I bet the dumb bastard never even heard of one or the other. Any dope knows the answers to those questions, but I wouldn't give him the satisfaction. I don't think he liked me because I was a shrimp and he had to lean over to talk to me. He was about six-five. On the Rorschach I really took him on a merry chase. So, I came out nuts. I screwed up all his other tests too. Maybe," Benny said after a moment, "maybe by screwing them up I proved I was nuts, huh?"

There were numerous instances of fugue states in Benny's experiences. Sometimes he would disappear and, according to his own reports, he would arrive someplace without ever knowing how he got there. On occasion he would run madly through the woods, as if to get away from some enemy. "They were always real at first," he said of these enemies. "But after a while, when I got tired and sat down, I realized nobody was after me and I'd cry like hell. That's when I'd either work like a madman on my stuff or I'd come down and talk to you for days on end. A few times when I couldn't get to you I'd go to a priest in the confessional, but I almost always made up stories for them. I couldn't see their eyes in that darkness anyway. I don't like to talk to eyeless people. And I guess I got into a bad habit of lying to priests when I was a kid. But I felt better anyway, even with the lies.

"But, you know, since I was a little kid I've always worried about myself. When I was three or four years old I remember having a number of dreams that repeated themselves over and over. They were frightening dreams, hard and dangerous dreams. I remember I was always walking along narrow paths on high mountains, looking down steep cliffs and canyons into the lonely and tempestuous sea below. Walking along these very narrow paths would often scare the hell out of me and I would at times find myself crying. I guess that's why I was attracted to the Big Sur, trying to find my dreams, even though I was afraid of them. Instead of dying with my boots on, I used to think that I would die from falling off one of those cliffs at the Big Sur. And, you know, many times I thought of suicide up there — like just letting myself fall off and drop down to the rocks and sea below. And I wondered if anybody would miss me, if I did.

"I never feared death. It was like Montaigne said: It is not death but the dying that alarms me. I always wanted to die fast and not linger along with an illness. Even though I've been a crook, even though I've been a big liar at times, even though I've deceived lots of people, I still feel that I'm a hell of a lot better person than ninety-nine percent of our other animal brethren. I never killed a man, an animal or a plant. I killed myself, though, many times. An artist is a strange character. He puts himself into his work, and if he doesn't like what he sees, he demolishes it. And when he does, he kills himself. And that's how I committed suicide.

"Sometimes I would go into a fury, but luckily I was able to control myself most of the time around people. You've seen some of the crazy things I have done. You know that I wrecked many of my statues and that I cleverly put the blame on vandals. It was because I hated myself so much. And when people found fault with my statues, it was the same as criticizing me. It hurt, hurt deep. It was like my father bawling me out all the time. I used to hate him, and when I met people like him in my life, I used to hate them too, most of the time without reason.

"I'm a man of peace, but underneath I'm also a man of war. I've had terrible feelings that I wanted to kill people sometimes, those who got in my way. But I was lucky. I had my work, and whenever I felt that way I would pound and hammer on my sculpture until I was a free man again. But sometimes, I couldn't do the right things with my material. It didn't give right. Then I would go and smash my other things. That Bach head you held for me for so long. The drippy nose. It wasn't my fault; things like that happen. But it ate my heart out. I couldn't bear having kids laugh at it, as I saw one day — a group of kids laughing at the snot dripping out of his nose, as they called it. It couldn't go on display for the world to make fun of. So, I demolished it in Carmel. I almost gave myself away to the press when I told them that only a guy who knew the workings of an armature could have dislodged the head. I sure thought they'd catch on.

"No one knew when I was coming to the festival. I sneaked down there one night — hitched actually — and killed myself, with the help of a prominent guy in San Francisco. It was really an accident, though. In taking it off I dropped the head. And nobody will ever find some of it — I pushed some pieces off into the ocean and others I hid along the road and in a park.

"That's another funny thing about me. I like to hide everything and yet I like to display things. I don't know what I'm doing sometimes. I don't know why I'm that way. It might have something to do with the distrust I have of people, with their deception. I've never really understood them — people I mean. They say one thing and act another way. And I guess I'm the same. I guess it's me that I hate so much in other people. But things drive me on sometimes. I really don't understand myself, and what worries me more than anything is that I think I'm such a phony sometimes."

Benny loved people but didn't trust them, not even his best friends. He made his statues so that people, kids in particular, could rub their hands over them and bring the warmth out of the cold granite or stainless steel. He believed that people should develop their sense of touch, but when others touched him personally he pulled away. He admitted that he was ashamed of his body, and when he undressed in the presence of men he allowed only his back to be seen. What he really did with women is a story that only the women in his life could tell, but he said in private that no woman had ever seen him naked except his mother, "and then I was too young to care.

"As you know, women have always bothered me. Somebody once told me that I could never find my mother in another woman, that's why I'd never get married. I was eighteen years old then, and it was a woman who told me that. Women always seemed so superior to men. I think of my mother and my father — I think of the Little Sister of the Stones — and in most of the families I know the woman is the superior one. And if a man takes time off to love a woman, he's doomed. He can never be creative with a woman around. She eats into his thoughts, into his bones. You're either a lover or an artist. You can't be both. Each time I got lost in a woman, my art suffered. So, I say, to hell with women.

"Then again, maybe it's not women who are at fault. It must be the man who is basically weak. I know it was true of me. As an adolescent I was scared of any girl who came near me. When I got my balls caught on the telephone-pole spike — it ruined me for the rest of my life.

"I was just a kid and I was trying to climb a pole. I slipped and got caught and hung upside down on that spike. That hurt me so much that I passed out, and when I came to, my uncle was up on the pole trying to get me untangled from my knotted pants. Dr. Tomasulo said I bled like a pig, too. Maybe that's why I've been scared to let a woman see me, or anyone.

"I was never a very sexy guy. In school, some of the guys must have thought I was a homo. The older, bigger guys used to play with my thigh and then grab my penis. I'd yell like hell, even in the classroom. Of course the teacher never knew what was going on. I pretended I had a bellyache and I'd scream more and more. I got out of school that way lots of times. I was always a good actor. You had to be in New York, or you'd get murdered.

"You ask how many wives I've had. Hell, I don't know, but I do know there weren't many. I think there were really three, or maybe four. In fact, I may be a bigamist, even more than once. I think I got married first in Pennsylvania — the town of Nanty Glo, I think it was — or maybe I thought I got married there because the name sounded romantic to me. As soon as I got married, I forgot about her. Marriage always gave me a headache and a complete loss of memory. I think I got married because I wanted to prove something — mainly to my father.

"When I first got married I didn't know what the hell to do with a woman. I said to her, 'Go ahead, I'm all yours.' I think she laughed so hard that she died in bed that night. I hardly remember after that, anyway. I think we got a divorce. My brother Tony arranged it. But hell, I was such a little guy — all over, even down there, you know. So, I have a natural doubt that I could ever have a kid of my own. I don't think I ever really got into a woman, but then sometimes I don't always remember everything. Sometimes I get blank spells. But then, how can a guy produce a kid when he's been de-nutted?

"Anyhow, I don't trust women. And when anybody asks about my Finnish girl friend, Tabe Slioor, all I can do is smile. You can't blame a guy for trying, for trying to catch up on lost time. Maybe it's second childhood. Whatever it is, I'm having a hell of a good time, and I have a lot of people guessing. I haven't even told her what I've got in mind. Maybe she'll reveal her side of the story someday. I won't. But then, whatever she's said to the newspapers has been a lot of crap. One thing I've learned about her is that I can't believe her, so nobody else can. I guess every man likes to have a little glamor about him. Maybe I was dumb fifteen years ago not to follow up on my contact with Zsa Zsa Gabor — she was more to my liking. And she liked my art, too. I think I met her through Raymond Burr, or Otto Preminger. Hell, my memory is really slipping."

Benny always emphasized in public that he was bankrupt, poverty-stricken, destitute. Yet, in the strict confidence of our "therapeutic" relationship — a confidence kept till now — Benny admitted he had buried almost $100,000 in different places around the world. "The worms will get most of it," he said one day about a year before his death. "Just so some of my greedy so-called friends won't get it. They'll be shocked when they hear it from you."

And at another time he had said: "I'm just like the worst money-grabbers in the world. I covet money. I must have power. And I hate those things worst in my friends or my enemies.

"You know the story about my money. Always the guy who lives on bread and water, the guy who has no money, the man who is the best example of the true artist. And sometimes, because you've known some things about me that others haven't, I have wanted to kill you. You'll never know, and maybe I won't either because maybe I'm telling a story to make an impression. But you'll never know how close you came to being killed after I first told you that we didn't have to worry about money.

"I felt sorry for you because you were a professor and weren't making much money. I had just seen Otto Preminger and Leon Shamroy, and I thought I would try to get you a job in the movies. You had such a large family to take care of, and then you would always take care of my expenses when I came down to Los Angeles. One time you took me out to dinner and didn't have enough to pay for it. I then said, 'Don't worry, I'll take care of it.' And you were shocked to learn that I had money.

"Hell, I've always had money. When I told you that, you looked amazed. I told you that I couldn't trust people, and the banks I could trust the least. So, I told you we would never have to worry about money, that I had money hid around the world. One guy, a real good guy by the name of Fratelli in San Fele, was one who knew where I had buried about $18,000. I took out some of the stones in the wall near the church and put the money there — money I had received from Liebes, Verdier, Moar and other guys to do my work, but which was more than I needed. I hated myself for that, I hated myself for taking money from other people who thought I was bankrupt and poverty-stricken.

"And you know about Anderson Creek in the Big Sur, where I have other money buried. In a place I call St. Francis in Mendocino County I have some more money buried in a tin box, not far from where I was working on my Hand. I guess I must have close to a hundred thousand bucks hidden around the world. I lost what I hid in Paris, though.

"So, don't give me away. I deserved every extra penny I got. Wealthy people should pay a fortune just to keep the artists in this world. I tried to get it honestly, but the wealthy guy always backs away at the last minute, so you have to promise him things to get the money, and since many wealthy people are greedy they'll give you money hoping to get more in return."

On one occasion he mentioned to the president of the Bufano Society that Otto Preminger was coming to visit Benny in his studio. "I need a few bucks," said Benny. "I've got a statue made to order for his personality. He'll be glad to give me $9000 for it. It cost me half that much anyway."

When Preminger and some of his friends came for the visit they were duly impressed with all of Bufano's works. As the producer prepared to leave, Benny said, "Wait a minute, I've got something you'll like." He brought out the statue and Preminger raved about it. Benny chuckled, his eyes gleamed.

"Benny," said Otto, "you don't know what this means to me. This is the most wonderful gift I've ever received." And he hugged Benny. On his way out, he said, "Thanks a million." For one of the few times in his life Benny was so stunned he couldn't utter a word, let alone say "You're welcome."

But Benny wasn't as hard-boiled about money as he wanted me to believe. Over the years he provided 17 struggling artists in the San Francisco area with more than $20,000, "so they could keep their heads above water. And some of them never knew where the money came from. And some of them fought the hardest against me when I was being attacked. It's a crazy world."

Benny had been hospitalized for a heart condition, although he never mentioned it. Many of Benny's friends thought he would live forever, and perhaps he felt that way, too. Bufano never stopped working.

"Anyhow, I've got lots of ideas. I'm working on the plans for that fifty-foot statue for Catalina. I really think it will be my greatest. Imagine all the ships and planes that pass over the island. They can use the statue of Cabrillo as a beacon, and so can all the yachtsmen coming over from the mainland. He was a great guy, Cabrillo. He was Portuguese, but he had a lot in common with me. I hope to have everything ready for Wrigley in about two weeks."

Ten days later Benny and his plans for Cabrillo were dead. On August 18, 1970, friends found his body on the floor near the bed in his San Francisco studio at 83 Minna Street. He was a victim of heart failure. His death certificate lists his age as 79, his date of birth as October 15, 1890.

According to columnist Herb Caen, one of Benny's better friends, $12.75 was found in his pockets — $11 in paper money and $1.75 in small change. Erskine Bufano, his only son, and Aloha Nielson, Benny's daughter, decided to use that $1.75 to buy themselves a drink in a San Rafael bar. They drank a toast to their late father and then retained attorney Vincent Hallinan to attempt to break Bufano's will, in which Erskine is not mentioned and Aloha is specifically excluded. "My father," adds Erskine, "was true to life even after death. His $1.75 wasn't quite enough to pay for the drinks."

Shortly after Benny's death, his son filed a petition in San Francisco Superior Court asking that he be appointed administrator of his late father's estate, his sole interest being to prevent the sale of Benny's works. However, his lawyer indicated that the will would be challenged, because Hallinan considered it to show "incompetence," since Benny stated that he had never been married, "and obviously he married twice."

Benny first made a will in 1944, revised it in 1955, and then reframed another in 1956, all of them holographic. The present, contested will was written in 1962 and amended in 1966, leaving his estate to the Bufano Society of the Arts, specifying that, if it were contested, two-thirds of the estate should go to the University of Santa Clara. The United California Bank was designated the executor but declined to act in that capacity, claiming that the estate consisted of disputed works of art, some controlled by the Bufano Society and others that Benny had given to his Finnish girl friend, Tabe Slioor. At present the will is up for grabs.

Benny Bufano is a legend. As a legend he does not exist except in memory. And as Benny played games with the facts, so does one's memory play games with the man that was. Underneath his sham, his facade and his many stories, what was he really like?

Truth is neither of CREED nor
Race

It is not of the STREET
It is not of The TEMPle

It is neither of DARkness
nor of Light
It is an Extenlion of the
Soul of man
In his adventure Beyond
Reality

Bear and Cubs, perhaps Bufano's best-known animal sculpture, is on display at the Hillsdale Shopping Center in San Mateo. Bufano's copies of the work may also be found at the Oakland Art Museum; the University of California Medical Center, San Francisco; and the Marin County Humane Society.

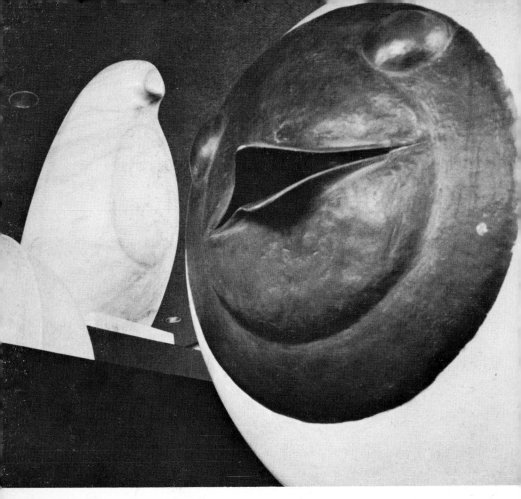

Of Bufano's animals at the Alcoa Building in San Francisco, this picture includes the bronze face of a yellow-marble blowfish and a rotund parrot all done in Bufano's smooth, rounded lines.

The Prayer, Bufano's penguin in stainless steel and red porphyry, was damaged in World War II when Aquatic Park was leased by the military. Benny restored the work, and it now stands in the Maritime Plaza, San Francisco.

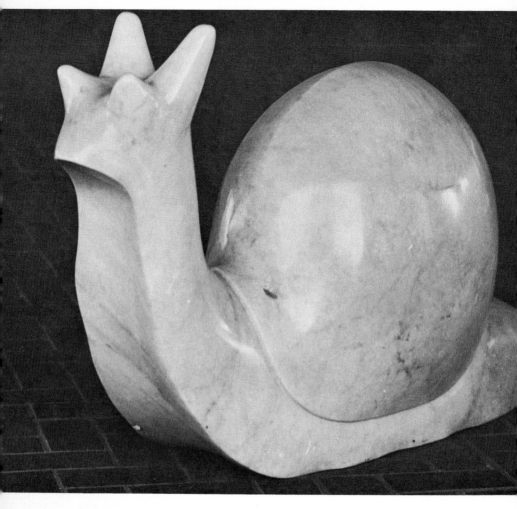

Bufano's snail lifts its head with dignity. The work is presently at the Alcoa Building.

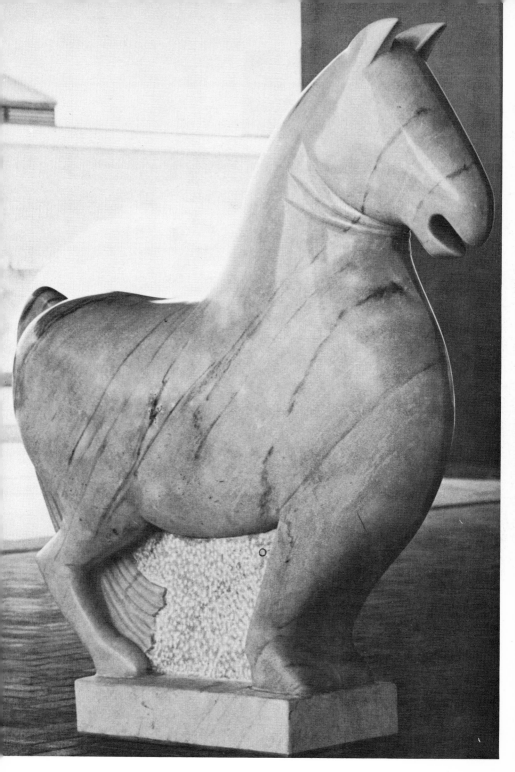

The horse, also at the Alcoa Building, displays the full power of Bufano's magic with stone: the diagonal striping of the marble lends seeming action.

The ungainly elephant attains a pleasing shape, rounded and smoothed to indicate the solid, rocklike quality of the beast. This work, too, is at the Alcoa Building.

At the Valencia Courts housing project in San Francisco, Bufano's mouse and rabbit have received casual treatment from the children. Rainwater dripping from the rabbit's eye has stained his cheek, which seems appropriate in view of the humiliating stickers.

These cats are reminiscent of the San Francisco Press Club's "Tombstone." The figure above is at the Hillsdale Shopping Center, the one below at the Alcoa Building. Bufano delighted in carving a peacefully sleeping mouse on the head of an owl or a cat, as on the statue above.

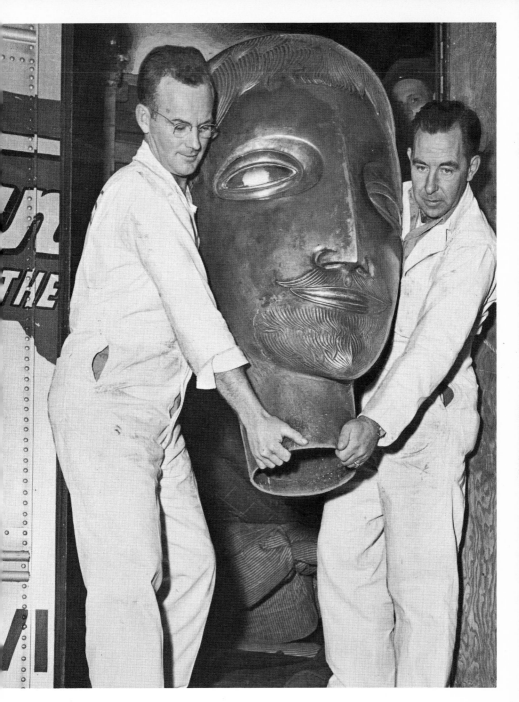

In 1955 workmen are moving the huge copper head of a St. Francis that Bufano gave to Stanford University.

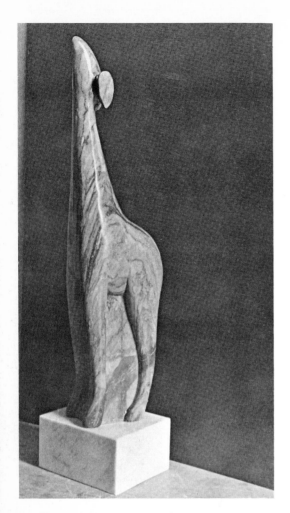

The giraffe and the parrot, both in marble, are examples of Bufano's "touchable" animals.

At the Hillsdale Shopping Center Bufano's sea lion lifts its head.

Bufano's marble duck is also at the Alcoa Building.

PEACE

BY
BENIAMINO BUFANO

Bufano's *Peace*, placed at the San Francisco International Airport in 1958, is of stainless steel, mosaic and black granite.

The last photograph ever taken of
Benny was made in early August, 1970.

PICTURE CREDITS

Authors' Collection: 19, 20, 96-98, 216, 228
William M. Drew: 85-90, 92-95, 99, 217-226, 229-231
Patrick Moore: jacket and frontispiece
San Francisco *Examiner*: 91, 100, 227, 232